SOCIOLOGY OF LITERATURE

Dedicated
to
Late Budrul-Hoda-Siddiqui
Dr. M.K.A. Siddiqui
and
Ali Arshad Siddiqui

SOCIOLOGY OF LITERATURE

(A Study of Urdu Novels)

SYED FAZLE RAB

Commonwealth

SOCIOLOGY OF LITERATURE

Edition : 2023

ISBN 81-7169-191-9

Published by :
COMMONWEALTH PUBLISHERS (P) LTD.
4831/24, Govind Lane,
Ansari Road, Darya Ganj,
New Delhi - 110002
Ph. : 23242541, 23272541
e-mail : commonwealthpublishers2016@gmail.com

Distributed by :
ARJUN PUBLISHING HOUSE
4831/24, Govind Lane,
Ansari Road, Darya Ganj,
New Delhi - 110002
Ph. : 23242541, 23272541
e-mail : arjunbooks2001@gmail.com

Laser Typesetting by :
Dimple Computers
Delhi

Printed at :
Balaji Digital
Delhi

Prefaec

The present study, is an attempt to investigate into the socio-cultural background of major urdu novels published in India during 1947-'67.

With the achievement of independence in the year 1947, the Indian people and society entered into a new phase and during the first twenty years or so they had to face different changes and challenges which can be very well obseved in the works of different urdu novelists, who more than other creative writers have concentrated on the fundamental questions and taken keen interests in social matters as well as problems of their time. Some eminent Urdu novelists like Krishan Chander, K.A. Abbas and Razia Sajjad Zaheer have traced the various factors of socio-economic exploitations in our contemporary society while others like Kazi Abdus Sattar, Quarratul-Ain-Haider etc. portray the picture of the decaying feudal aristocracy. Thus the urdu novels, like the novels in other languages, can be considered as the 'living source books' which provide us with a valid insight obout the important sociological matters like the social groups and their interaction, the pattern and extent of mobility, social change etc. In this sense the Urdu novels are suited to sociological investigations.

The selection of novels in this study has been done on a random basis and only those novels were taken which became popular during the period under study.

I am indebted to Dr. Dipti Kumar Biswas, Professor of Sociology, Bhagalpur University, Bhagalpur for inspiring me to take up this project. Dr. Biswas was the first scholar to make sociological study of Bengali Novels in the country.

I am also grateful to my father Late Dr. S.M. Ismail, Rtd, S.D.O. Education, my mother Mrs. Tahera Khatton, my wife Dr. Seemen Samar Fazal, Asstt. Librarian, Sinha Library,

Patna, Budruddoja, Dr. Sharaf, Shamuzzoha, Shaheen and Mimshad for their co-operation and encouragement in carrying out this work.

Lastly, I must also record my deep sense of appreciation for Nishat, Taha and Saba who compelled me to get this manuscript published which I prepared several years back. However, I owe my limitations.

Syed Fazle Rab

Contents

1

Introduction

Analysing literature is a fascinating approach which is being developed in sociology. Sociology of literature can be treated as a legitimate branch of ever-increasing science of society. The present study endeavours to analyse the socio-cultural background of urdu novels—one of the most popular forms of literary art. While introducing the subject matter of the present work it is felt necessary to provide an acquaintance with the meaning of the sociology of literature, the evolution of urdu literature and the dominant socio-cultural themes of the period covered by the present study viz., the post independence period.

A. SOCIOLOGY OF LITERATURE

Literature may be defined as the representation of life through the medium of a social creation viz., language. The writer endeavours to communicate his conception of life : Life as he sees it. Human life is, therefore, the raw material for literature; human joys and sorrows, human aspirations and ideals, human virtues and vices, human greatness and degradation are the stuff of which it is made. "Whatever the form—poem, novel, drama, biography essay—literature makes comprehensible myriad ways in which human beings meet the infinite possibilities that life offers."[1] According to Hudson "literature is a vital record of what men have seen in the life,

1. Rosenblatt, Louis M. : "Literature as exploration", London, p. 6, Heinemann Educational Books Ltd., 1970.

what they have thought and felt about those aspects of it, which have the most immediate and enduring interest for all of us. It is thus fundamentally an expression of life through the medium of language."[2] Thus literature is a mirror of life, a reproduction, a social document which has, "peculiar merit of faithfully recording the features of the times and of perserving the most picture-sque and expressive representation of manners."[3]

Relationship between literature and social order poses a major problem and involves different issues viz., their interdependence, relative significance, the question of an independent existence of literature and the like, which are not easily answerable. Outwardly literature is concerned with beauty and inwardly related to welfare and truth. It enriches itself by accommodating the social trends and at the same time maintains the special features of the place of its origin.

Man is a social animal and also the creator of literature. This may be considered as the significant reason for the relationship between the two. The norms and values of the different societies are reflected in their respective literatures and this creates regional differences. But men and their societies all over the world bear some common elements which enable them to understand and appreciate the literature of one another. The genius is never confined to any limit. They are above their countries and ages. We get some eternal tunes in their works. Literature, therefore, is a social phenomenon. It is a product of society as it develops only in a social context, as a part of a culture. "It is an integral part of the entire culture tied by a tissue of connections with every other elements in the culture."[4]

A writer takes his literary raw materials from society and washes them in the powerful emotional stream of his

2. Hudson, W.T. : "An introduction to the study of Literature", p. 10, London, George G Herper, 1958.
3. Warren, Austin and Wellek, Rene. : "Theory of literature", London, Jonathan Cap, 1954.
4. 'Selections from the Encyclopedia of the Social `ciences;' N.Y. ; The Macmillan Co., 1959.

personality. As a matter of fact, "the range of social influences on literature is as broad as the entire range of operative social forces; the prevailing system of social organization—including the class structure; the economic system, the political organizations; the dominant ideas, the characteristics and emotional tone, the sense of the past and the pattern of future, the deriving aspiration and myths and their relation to contemporary realities."[5] That is why there is a marked difference between the novels, plays, and poems of the present time and those of century ago. The early literature laid greater stress on ethics and emphasised upon the need for reforming the character and moral of the people but the process has now changed. The modern literature has become more materialistic in approach and defines the human actions as related to the economic and social factors.

Literature differs from one nation to another, and from one social system to another. Every society has its own norms of behaviour as well as different problems and anxieties. Each society, also, sets some kind of goal. A country, like India, which is based on secular and democratic ideals provides different themes and contents to literature in comparison to literature of a communist country, like China, where there is no freedom of speech and expression, thus literature develops under different social, political and economic conditions, but the kind and quality of literature depends on the conditions of the society.

Geographical environment also, in some way, determines the shape and character of literature, particularly novel and drama. Thus literature of a society is coloured with the images, figures and forms most often taken from the geographical environment in which such a society functions. According to Sorokin "The Thousand and One Nights or the Illiad and Odyssy, or the Norse Edda, or the Hindu Mahabharatha are quite different from each other and each is marked by the characters typical of the locality in which its creator lived."[6]

5. Ibid , p. 524.
6. Sorokin, Pitirim : 'Contemporary Sociological Theories' New York, Harper, & Row, Publisher, 1964, p. 171.

Literature is also influenced by scientific development and inventions. Science not only provides new thoughts and contents to literature but also determines its new directions. Twentieth century is remarkable for a series of discoveries in the fields of science and technology. The techniques of birth control, nuclear energy, lethal weapons etc. are some of developments in the fields of science and technology which have revolutionised the society as well as its value structure. A writer reveals these problems and anxieties of his age. The earlier stories dealt mostly with supernatural, mythological adventures and were stereotyped in nature. But the modern scientific and technological advancements have changed the themes and treatments of the stories. The concept of imaginative literature has become a difficult matter in our science oriented dynamic society.

The modern scientific and technological inventions have enormously changed the status and position of women. She is no more a machine for child-bearing and child-rearing but she has become an important part of the society. She works in industries, mills, workshops, hotels, aeroplanes, educational institutions, and holds key positions in politics and government. Hence, unlike early stories, the female characters of contemporary novels are doctors, nurses engineers, airhostesses, sales-girls, legal practitioners, social workers, receptionists, teachers, political leaders and government servants etc. But the novels of a few decades back revealed quite different picture of the women folk.

Scientific inventions and discoveries have made the world smaller. The rapid growth of mass media of communications has linked up the entire population of the world. An incident in any part of the world may affect all. This impact of science has helped the writers to produce the humanitarian literature based on international understandings.

The form and style of literature are linked with culture of the society. Literature reflects the changes which take place within culture. Literature is a symbolic expression of a culture and it changes according to the change in culture. In order to communicate about what man perceives around him the writer uses symbols. The basic aim of symbols which stand for the objects of our experience is to identify and define them to ourselves and others. All social processes and all societal forms are based on the transfer of meaning between individuals, and social life exists only because meaningful symbols are transferred from individual to individual and from group to group. In fact, no group activities can be carried on without a means to share experiences. This concept has been defined by Cooley as "... the mechanism through which human relations exist and develop all the symbols of the mind; together with the means of conveying through space and preserving them in time."[7] As a matter of fact the writer creates these symbols not only in a specific form, characteristic of his personality, and manner, but also in the specific form of his time and his society, in the style of his period. According to Egon E. Bergel, "Style is never the creation of a single person: many contribute to its emergence and the artist, although he is not forced to do so, adopts the style of his age and group. Style is thus an eminently social phenomena... style in some way expresses the philosophy, the feelings and the values of a generation. This, too, is a social phenomena and in great need of scientific analysis and explanation."[8]

If literature is influenced by social forces and social processes, on the other hand, it also affects the existing norms and behaviours of the people in a society. It changes the attitudes and opinions of individuals and determines new trends and directions of the social values. It criticises the ethical standard of the society and stimulates the people to revolt against useless ethics. The literature not only reveals the problems and anxieties of the age but it also explains the reasons behind them. In all civilised societies of the world literature is adorned because it explains the contemporary social condition and their problems. The great literary creations are those which reveal

7. Cooley, C.H. : 'Social organization' New York, Charles Scribners' & Sons, 1909, p. 51.
8. Bergel, Egon E. : 'Prolegomena to Sociology of Art' 'Towards sociology of culture in India'. Ed. by T.K.N. Unithan et al New Delhi, Prentice Hall of India (Private) Ltd., 1965, p. 110.

the social, religious, economic and domestic values of their times and the authors of such works also become immortals like Balmiki, Kalidas, Shakespear, Milton, Iqbal, Ghalib, Tagore and others. The writings of Rousseau and Voltaire created an atmosphere for the emergence of the forces of Industrial Revolution in France. Gorky, Tolstoy and Chekov brought revolution in Russia through their impressive writings. In the same way the writings of Gandhi, Gokhle, and Azad helped us in achieving the independence of India. The religious literature of the past changed the destiny of human beings by provoking new ideas and thoughts. During the Indo-Pak and Indo-China wars writers could inspire the sense of patriotism and unity in the hearts of Indians through their writings and enabled us to foil the aggressive motives of the invaders.

Literature acts as one of the agencies in our culture that transmits images of behaviour, emotions, attitudes, social and ethical standards. It suggests the socially approved beneficial channels for expression of our impulses. Literature plays an important role as a process through which the individual becomes assimilated into his cultural pattern. Literary experiences enable the reader to view his own personality and problems objectively and so to handle them in a better way. It introduces the adolescents to the diversity of the possible way of life, patterns of relationship, and different ideologies from which he is free to choose in a heterogenous and rapidly changing democratic society.

To a human being the most interesting phenomenon is the human life itself. The literature which analyses, explains, and provides solution to the problems of human life becomes much attractive to us. It is something like a written argument submitted to the judiciary within us for self defence. We appologise for our wrong steps in literature, defend our actions and movements and at the same time give explanations for our shortcomings. Literature, therefore, acts as a measure of self defence. A particular branch of knowledge, for example Mathematics, which has nothing to do with human heart can not be considered as literature. Human life has a vest span and so also the enquiries about it. They cover the entire universe and constitute the real domain of literature.

Literature and art are the two medias through which the society and the life of the individual can be expressed. But literature is more effective in comparison to the art because though the artist can draw a portrait of, say an angry man, he can not, like a literature, give an explanation for the anger. In other words the literature explains the reason behind the state of mind. In this capacity literature excels art. Literature is adorned in all the civilised societies of the world because it explains the contemporary social conditions. The great literary creations to mention once again; are those which contain the social themes of their period and the authors of such works also become immortals.

Sociology of literature thus deals with the relationship between the literature and the components of social order or culture, literary themes and structure, process of integration and cleavage in relation to the types of social structure, as well as the level of adjustment and changes. The study of literature as a social phenomenon can be found in the writings of a number of social thinkers and critics. Three general assumptions are that literature reflects society and culture; that it serves as a means of social control; and that it influences attitudes and behaviour of people.

In 1800, Madame de Stael began to discuss the relation of race and climate to literary styles, as well as the effects of women and religion on art. "In her view literature should portray important changes in the social order, especially those which indicate movement towards the goals of liberty and justice. Her writings on this topic had wide influence during her life and few decades after."[9]

As early as 1845 Karl Marx also provided a more specific thesis concerning the relation of literature and society. According to Marx the system of production in existence at a given time determines both the content and the style of the literature of a society.[10] The Marxian analysis of the interrelations of

9. Quoted by James H. Barnett : 'The Sociology of Art': Sociology to-day : Problems and Prospects' Ed. by Robert K. Merton etc. New York, Basic Books Inc., 1959, p. 199.

10. Marx, Karl and Engels, Frederick : 'Literature and Art', New York, International Publishers, 1947.

literature and society was of value because it specified the particular aspect of a society that might affect its art and insisted on a continuous, dynamic interchange among all parts of that society. A host of scholars representing a wide range of intellectual committments to Marxist sociology, have adopted this point of view in studying literature and their views have been influential. In Europe Lukacs and Caudwell, although they did not accept Marx's transcedent proleteterian, adopted Marxist theories of social class in their analyses of art. Huizingas also used art works and art theory for interpretation of society.[11]

Herbert Spencer explained the origin of art in terms of conditioning effects of a specific stage of social adaptation. According to him human beings have the capacity to accumulate more energy than is necessary for servival.[12] In the course of evolutionary development, the extra energy became the basis for developing leisuretime activities which yield enjoyment. With an increase in the availability of unused energy the volume of art also expands in human society. However, his thesis accounted only for the origin of arts as a part of culture and did not enable scholars to explain difference in its form and content. It stimulated discussion of art from a naturalistic point of view.

Hippolyte Taine's work, 'History of English Literature' (1871) gave a new approach for the study of literature. According to him "A work of art is determined by an aggregate which is the general state of mind and surrounding circumstances."[13] He sought to account for this state of mind through the application of analytical formula—"race-environment-time"——to different countries. The term 'race' comprehsended sets

11. Duncan, Hugh D.—Sociology of art. literature and Music : social contexts of symbolic experience, "Modern sociological theory in continuity and change" Ed. by Howard Beeker Alvin, Boskoff. New York, Rine Heart and Winston, 19?7, p. 484.

12. Spencer, Herbert, "The principles of Psychology", New York, Appleton, 1882, Vol. III, pp. ?29 f.

13. Taine, Hippolyte, "History of English literature" New York, Henry Holt, 1886, Vol. I, p. 30.

of ideas about heredity, land and climate; 'environment' included social, economic and cultural factors; while 'time' focused attention on aspects of both stability and change in a civilization. Thus his detailed application and discussion of his proposition made it apparent that he attached special importance to the social medium or milieu which produces the 'state of mind', necessary for artistic creation.

In 1887, Jean-Maric Quyan, a French Scholar, in his thesis 'Art from the point of view of sociology' claimed that social integration is embodied in works of art. He provided few alternatives for the studying of art and society and gave interesting and valuable analysis of social ideas embodied in the work of Victor Hugo, Alfred de Vigny, Alfred de Musset and other important French writers. Quyan's writings on the relation of art to the social environment influenced too many French Scholars and critics.

During the 20th century, sociologists interested in the relation of literature and society have undertaken both theoretical discussions and specific research in this field. "Durkheim and Max Weber, although they dealt primarily with religious experience, created theoretical and methodological tools for the analysis of art and play... By the end of twenties, hermeneutics, the study of symbolic interpretation, was a well defined field in the writing of Wach and Cassirer. Marx and Weber taught us, further, that men use art in the struggle for power among classes. Malinowski summed up anthropological views in his description of myth as kind of social charter" [14] But the most important and extensive work in this field is Sorokin's social and cultural dynamics'. Sorokin believes that he has discovered abundant evidence to explain that several arts fluctuate in time between two polar conceptual type—the ideational and the sensate. "The literary work which deals with the invisible world, supernatural and transcendental, and in which words and images are but symbols of this world, is, according to definition, Ideational literature. The work which depicts and describes empirical phenomena in their sensory

14 Duncan, Hugh D. Op. cit., p. 482.

aspects, where words and images have nothing but empirical meaning, is sensate literature."[15]

Freud also opened up several avenues for the sociologist of literature. In "Wit and the unconscious" he stressed the need for analysing reciprocal relations between author and public in terms of status as well as of sexual concepts. By 1945 Burke gave a synthesis of Marx, Frazer and Freud into a fully developed theory. "In a rounded statement about motives, you must have some world that names the act (names what took place in thought or deed), and another that names the scene (the background of the act, the situation in which it occurred); also you must indicate what person or of person (agent) performed at the act, what means or instrument he used (agency), and the purpose."[16]

Thus Burke offers us with a specifically sociological theory, precise enough in formulation, to allow us to develop analytical tools for the investigation of literary works. "Art work must be analysed in terms of what dramatic struggle goes on, under what conditions, by what means, between what kinds of actors, or in what kinds of actions, and for what purpose. This is done by showing how, in the form and content of art work itself, values held inimical to the survival of the society are destroyed, as in the symbolic killing of the villain; how values held necessary to the survival of the group are preserved of brought into being, as in the symbolic birth, rebirth or victory of the hero."[17]

In 1954, a study has been made by Kolaja and Wilson for the investigation of painting and poetry in relation to social environment. The authors examine the possibility that different art media of a given society will exhibit certain common cultural characteristics at a particular time.[18]

15. Sorokin Pitirim, : Social and cultural dynamics, Fluctuations of form of art, New York, American Book, 1937, p. 187.
16. Burke, Kenneth. : 'A Grammar of motives' New York, Prentice-Hall, 1945, p XV.
17. Duncan, Hugh D. : Op. cit., p. 488.
18. Kolaja, Jiri and Wilson, Robert N. : 'The themes of social isolation in American painting and poetry' Aesthetics and art criticism, pp. 37-45.

B. EVOLUTION OF URDU LITERATURE

India is a country with multi-languages and multidialects. Urdu is one of the fifteen languages of India.[19] The origin of urdu language, like other languages, is not quite accidental rather it is the result of various social, cultural and political forces which were taking place just after the arrival of Muslims in this country.

There are many views regarding the origin of urdu. Mohammad Hussain Azad wrote that urdu was the product of Brij Bhasha and Brij Bhasha was the main language of India.[20] Maulana Syed Sulaiman Nadvi says that urdu was brought into existence with the amalgamation of Arabic and Sindhi.[21] Another view has been given by Prof. Mahmud Sherani that the origin of urdu took place in the land of five rivers viz., the Punjab.[22] Nasiruddin Hashmi writes that mother land of urdu is Daccan and Wajdi, according to him, was the first urdu poet.[23] But all these views of the different scholars have been rejected by the modern scholars of linguistics such as Greirson, Dr. Suniti Kumar Chatterji, and Dr. Masood Hussain Khan. According to these scholars urdu is neither an off spring of persian or Brij Bhasha nor it has been born in the Punjab or the Daccan, but it was the Khariboli—a local dialect of Delhi and its neighbourhood—which was responsible for the birth of urdu language. Grierson has given a new name to Khariboli as 'Hindostani'.[24] According to Rambabu Saksena, "It is a dialect of the Western India Hindi spoken

19. Gazetter of India, Vol. II : Country and People, New Delhi, Publications Divisions, 1965, p. 373.
20. Azad, Mohammad Hussain, : 'Abe-Hayat', Ehsan Book Depot, p. 1.
21. Quoted by Mohammadullah Khan, Aligarh, Adeeb (6) June, 1959, p. 28
22. Ibid.
23. Ibid.
24. Grierson, George Abraham, : Linguistic Survey of India, Vol. I, Part I, p. 164, Calcutta, Govt. of India, Central Publication Branch, 1927.

for centuries in the neighbourhood of Delhi and Meerut and directly descended from 'Saur Senic Prakrit."[25]

The urdu language—its evolution, conception, and growth through an unconscious process—is the resultant of inter communication between the governors and the governed. The process of formation of the new language, urdu, bagan in Punjab with the invasions of Mahmud Gazni who occupied it in 1027 A.D. With the advent of Mahmud a great change took place over the local dialects because a large number of persian words began to be used frequently by the local people. Persian scholars also diverted their attentions towards the study of Indian culture and language. For instance, Al-Beruni of Khiva (973-1048 A.D.) came to India and studied the Indian customs and traditions, beliefs and faiths and different social institutions. During the reign of Qutub-Uddin Aibek, the slave king, Delhi became the centre of cultural activities and a large number of people from different parts of the country, especially from Lahore and Punjab, began to migrate to Delhi. At that time 'Khariboli', as mentioned above, an offshoot of western Hindi, was spoken in Delhi and its neighbourhood. The soldiers and people met and this interaction among the people belonging to two different linguistic gruops gave birth to a new common language with the amalgamation of Arabic, Persian, Turkish and Khariboli. In the beginning it was confined to conversation only, but "for the first time Khariboli", says Dr. Masood Hussain Khan, "was changed into the Persian script by Muslims."[26] In 1325 A.D. Mohammad Tughluk ascended to the throne of Delhi. He issued an order for the transfer of capital to Devagiri which was named as Daulatabad (Deccan). This transfer of capital made the situation congenial for the development of urdu. The language spoken in Delhi and its neighbourhood was transferred to Deccan where it was introduced to the local dielects of south and in course of time, a new language grew

25. Saksena, Rambabu, : A History of Urdu Literature. Allahabad, Ram Narain Lal, 1927, p. 1.
26. Khan, Masood Hussain, : Aligarh History of Urdu Literature, Vol. 1, Chapt. 1, p. 37.

in the form of 'Dakhini' which subsequently was named as urdu.

The religious preachers of Islam in this country also played an important role in the development of the new language by giving their patronage to it. "The subject matter of the earlier writings in urdu literature was religion and some of them were written nearly 400 years before there was any regular urdu composition in Delhi."[27]

During the closing years of the 16th century five small kingdoms ruled by muslim rulers had sprang up in the Deccan. The Adil Shahi (1490—1688) and the Qutub Shahi (1518—1687) were the two prominent dynasties which patronised urdu language and scholars. Mohammad Qutub Shah, the 4th King of the Qutub Shahi Dynasty (1580—1611), was himself a remarkable writer in both Persian and Urdu. The progress of urdu in Northern India remained very slow till the time of the Mughal Emperor Shah Jahan (1628 A.D.). During the reigns of Akbar and Jahangir the progress of urdu language was stoped due to the change of capital from Delhi to Agra where 'Brij Bhasha' was spoken. But in 1647 A.D. when Shahjahan changed his capital and organised the city of Delhi, Brij Bhasha lost its influence in the royal court and urdu became the centre of attration. The first urdu Ghazal (Poem) in Northern India was composed by *Pandit Chandra Bhan Brahaman* (1574—1662 A.D.) during the time of Shahjahan, though it was still in the rudimentary stage.

During the reign of Aurangzeb (1658—1707) a significant change took place in the form of urdu language and it was called 'Zuban-e-urdu' (the language of army) or Zuban-e-urdu-e-Mualla (the language of exalted or Royal Army) which up-rooted the influence of Brij Bhasha and adopted Persian style. Many Persian poets began to compose verses in the language of 'Rekhta' (a Persian word meaning poured but in India it was used for the urdu literary language) such as Mirza Musvi Khan Fitrat, Shah Sadullah Gulshan, Mirza Bedil, and Khan

27. Baily, T. Grahaime : Urdu Literature, Calcutta, Associated Press, 1932, p. 15.

Arzu.[28] But the fullfledged urdu literary activities started in Delhi at the arrival of Wali (1667—1741), a remarkable poet of Aurangabad (Deccan).

After the death of Aurangzeb (1707) and during the reigns of later Mughals urdu literature developed smoothly and reached its climax. Though it was the age of socio-economic and political upheavals but that did not affect adversely the onward march of urdu literature in India. The later Mughals were not only the patrons of urdu literature but were also worth mentioning poets of their time. For instance, Shah Alam II (1761—1806) was familiar with the Arabic and Persian also well versed in Turki and Hindustani languages,[29] and produced a masnavi (romance), known as 'Mazmun-i-Agolas' containing the story of Muzzaffar Shah, king of China.[30] Similarly Akbar Shah II (1806—1837) and Bahadur Shah Zafar (1837—1854) both were urdu poets. Mohammad Shah (1719—1748) was a great patron of art and literature. During his early peaceful regime a large number of urdu poets assembled in Delhi and founded a particular school of urdu literature known as "Delhi School of Urdu". Abru (d. 1750), Mazhar (1698—1781), Naji (d. 1754) and Yakrang were all the representatives of the Delhi School of Urdu Literature.[31] The growth of urdu literature was accelarated and Sauda (1713—1780), Mir (1724—1810), Dard (1719—1785), Mir Soz (1720—1798), Mir Hasson (1736—1786), Nazir (1740—1830) were some of the distinguished urdu poets of that age. They developed various forms of urdu poetry such as Ghazals, Qasida and Masnavi which revealed social, cultural and political awareness of their age.

In 1739 Nadir Shah gave a heavy blow to the reign of Mohammad Shah and as a result Delhi was turned in to a hell. Soon after that Ahmad Shah Abdali invaded India repeatedly between 1748 and 1761. These incursions as well

28. Op. cit. : Khan, Masood Hussain p. 173.
29. Jean Law (a French adventurer) quoted by Oxford History of India, p. 42.
30. Saksena, Ram Babu, : Op. cit , p. 96.
31. Faroqui, K.A. : Indian Literature, Ed. by Dr. Nagendra, p. 576.

as the growing power of the Marathas and their frequent raids of Northern India disturbed the tranquility of the country.

As a result of social and political chaos and unrest a large number of urdu poets left Delhi to seek asylum in the courts of Nawabs and Maharajas in the different parts of the country such as Lucknow, Hyderabad, and Azimabad (Patna). Lucknow was nearer to Delhi, naturally, Sauda, Mir, Mir Hassan, Soz and many others migrated there. At that time Asafuddalah was the Nawab of Oudh. He was very much generous to the poets of Delhi and provided all sorts of facilities and extended his patronage to them. In the same way other later Nawabs of Oudh viz. Wazir Ali khan, Saodat Ali Khan (1798—1814), Charaghuddin Haider (1814—1827), Nasiruddin Haider (1827—1837) and Wajid Ali Shah (1847—1856) gave the same treatment to the urdu poets and scholars of their times. Consequently, as mentioned earlier under the leadership of Nasikh and Atish, another school of urdu literature was established known as 'Lucknow school of urdu literature.

The social, economic and political conditions of the country under the later Mughals, the Nawabs, the Marathas, and the Sikhs declined to a great extent. In such a state of affairs the Britishers got an opportunity to increase their political power. They came here with an intention to establish factory but, "The factory grew into a fort, the fort expanded to a district and the district to a province, and then came collisions with less civilized neighbours, injuries to be resented, attacks to be repelled, and conflicts which always ended in victory and extension of territory."[32] Thus a new change in the political power came with the extenation of the kingdoms of Oudh and Delhi and the consolidation of British rule in India. Urdu literature could not escape the influence of these events of farreaching importance. During the rule of the Britishers a remarkable change was brought with the foundation of 'Fort William' College at Calcutta in 1800. This

32. Lord Palmerston (Debate in the British Parliament (Commons) vide Hansard, 12-2-1858, p. 1276).

college, under the able guidance of Gilchrist was started to enable the British officials to learn the local languages for the purpose of administration.

After the Mutiny, in 1857, a new wave of change emerged in the Indian society. It was an age of reformation and the wave of reformation was perceived both among the Hindus and the Muslims.

The Muslim reformers like their Hindu counter parts viz. Ram Mohan Roy, Swami Dayanand, Ishwar Chandra, Pandita Ram Bai, Annie Besant, Madan Mohan Malaviya and others started movements to improve the social, political, religious and economic status of Muslim community in the country. For instance, Sayyid Ahmad of Bareilly, Mirza Ghulam Ahmad and Sir Sayyid Ahmad Khan devoted their entire energy to change the intellectual, political and economic destiny of Indian Muslims. Sir Sayyid Ahmad (1817—1898) was very much influenced by the Western way of living and education. As a result of his efforts an Anglo-Mohammadan Oriental College was founded in 1875 at Aligarh. In 1870 he started an urdu journal 'Tahzib-ul-Akhlaq' modelled on Addison's 'Spectator' and Steel's 'Talter' which revolutionized urdu journalism, simplified urdu prose, and gave it a capacity to convey novel intellectual concepts in easily readable language.[33] In 1862 he founded a literary and scientific society at Ghazipur for translating English books into Urdu. In 1886 also founded he the Mohammadan Anglo-oriental conference and stressed upon the exercise of political pressure for the acceptance of urdu as the secondary language in all government and private schools. He also advocated for publishing and translating books into urdu. His movement the "Aligarh Movement" is so called because it centered around Aligarh Mohammadan Anglo-oriental collage founded by him."[34] Thus under the leadership of Sir Sayyid Ahmad Khan a new trend started in urdu literature. A large number of his contemporaries and followers such as Chiragh Ali (1844—

33. Ahmad, Aziz, Islamic Modernity in India and Pakistan 1957-1964, London, Oxford University Press, 1967, p. 38.
34. Encyclopaedia Britannica. Op. cit. p. 573.

1895), Mohammad Hussain Azad (d. 1910), Viqarul Mulk (1839-1917), Hali (1837-1914), Muhsinul Mulk (1837-1907), Shibli (1857-1914), Nazir (1831-1912) and Zakaullah (1832-1910) followed the same path and enriched the urdu literature by writing various social, political and religious themes in "Good, flowing and simple Urdu."[35]

Sir Sayyid on the other hand was opposed by an hostile group who did not share in 'Aligarh Movement' rather criticised the educational programme of Sir Sayyid Ahmad Khan through different platforms. "The organ of the opposition was the humorous journal 'Oudh Punch' (1877-1913), and its most effective weapon the witty satirical verse of Akbar (1846-1912). Oudh Punch did not share Aligarh's enthusiasm for British rule, and assailed it for trying to turn Indians into Englishmen."[36] Hence this opposition group also contributed much to the urdu literature which was used against Sir Sayyid and his followers.

With the beginning of the 20th century these forms and themes of literature took another shape and was deeply influenced by the various socio-economic and political forces which were emerging at home and abroad. "The main political ideas of the age-nationalism, Pan-Islamism, Muslim Communalism and finally, after 1917, Socialism and Communism—all influenced Urdu literature, which after 1900, and more especially 1918, enormously extended its range."[37]

The spirit of nationalism and freedom was being inculcated under the leadership of Gokhale, Tilak, Surender Nath Banerjee, Satayendra Nath and Firoz Shah Mahta among the Indian People but the 'Freedom Movement took its serious shape at the arrival of Mahatma Gandhi from South Africa in 1914. It was fortunate for India that the persons like Nehru, Jinnah, Azad, Patel and Bose came to the political arena and participated in non-cooperation movement, Swadeshi movement and formed the Swaraj Party. On the other hand

35. Ahmad, Aziz, Op. cit., p. 97.
36. Encyclopedia Britanaica. Op. cit., p. 573.
37. Encyclopedia Britannica, Op. cit., p. 573.

the introduction of western education created an impression upon the minds and actions of the contemporary generation and the western education enabled them to know about the profound thinkers and men of literature of the Western countries like Becon, Darwin, Marx, Freud, Spencer, Locke, Godwin, Mill, Adam Smith, Cerlyle, Ruskin, Ricardo, Gorky, Goethe, Victor Hugo, Zola, Balzac and many others. Consequently this contact expanded the outlook and added new dimensions to the thought and pattern of expression of the men of literature in our land. In the first few decades of the 20th century political romanticism was the dominating theme in Urdu literature which was emerging due to the aggression of western empires in Moroco, Persia and the Ottoman dominions, the extension and consolidation of French control in North Africa and especially Italy's occupation of Tripoli and the Balkan war of 1912 A.D.[38] Shibli composed the powerful topical poems full of rage and anguish at the aggression of western powers and later on Mohammad Ali and Hasrat Muhani, Chakbast, Iqbal and many others depicted the political theme with ths deep sense of patriotism in urdu literature. Thus urdu writers did not fail to record the feelings of the masses as the freedom movement acquired a higher tempo.

In the thirties various factors such as social and economic exploitation, Scientific innovations and attacks of communism, brought new trends in the modern urdu literature. As a matter of fact 'Progressive Movement' in urdu literature was started in 1936.[39] All writers were affected by it in one way or the other. "This new literature or progressive literature had at first both Marxist and Freudian trends in it. But very soon the two influences were separated from one another. Those who were influenced by Marx stood for social responsibilities and political awakening. They stood for man in the society, for the group, for an emotional approach to the march of history,

38. Represented in several anthologies such as Illyas Barani Ed. "Maarif-i-Millat", Aligarh, in 6 Vols.

39. Encyclopedia Britannica, Op. cit., p. 573.

for the progress of science, for an optimism in the fate of man in his struggle to break through the chains forged by feudalism and later on by capitalism .... The other group had less faith in tradition. It wanted complete freedom of literature both from traditional themes and prevalent diction".[40] Noteworthy among urdu writers and poets who were associated with this trend, were Josh, Firaq, Ali Sardar Jaferi, Majaaz, Makhdum and Faiz; the critics Majnun, Ihtisham Hussain Suroor; and the fiction writers Krishan Chandar, Minto, Bedi, Hayat Ullah Ansari, Ismat Chughtai, K.A. Abbas, Ashk, Sajjad Zaheer and many others.

After the partition of India urdu literature faced many challenges. Urdu was listed among the 14 (now 15) national languages in the Eighth Schedule of the Indian Constitution.[41] But urdu which played a prominent role in the freedom struggle became the victim of communalism. Leaders of the Muslim league, in pursuance of their early stand, tried to present urdu as the Lingua Franca of Pakistan. Consequently urdu lost its position in India and it was treated as the language of Muslims alone. Unfortunately, its vociferous advocacy by Muslim league and other communal organizations had given sustenance to this wrong impression though, both Hindus and Muslims have contributed to the evolution of urdu and its enrichment. Once Pandit Jawahar Lal Nehru said that "Urdu is an Indian language; it is a language of our country and even if there is not a single Muslim in India urdu will remain our cherished language."[42] In spite of many challenges, the progress of urdu literature during this period is a manifold phenomenon. It has made headway in many fields; in some of them the progress has been steady and

40. Suroor, A.A. : In contemporary Urdu Poetry. Transactions of the Indian Institute of Advanced Study : Modernity and Contemporary in Indian Literature, Simla, Indian Institute of Advanced Study, 1968, pp. 195-96, Vol. 5.
41. Gazetteer of India—Op. cit., p. 373.
42. Quoted by S.K. Zaidi in 'Urdu in India' : Problems and Prospects. "Transactions of Indian Institute of Advanced Study : Language and Society in India, Simla, Indian Institute of Advance Study, 1969, p. 236.

swift, in others hesitant and jerky. After independence the communal riots which followed it, emerged as the main topic of the period. Among Krishan Chandar's collection, 'Ham Wahshi Hain', Bedi's 'Lajwanti' and Hayat-ullah Ansari's 'Maa Aur Beta' are remarkable. A number of writers also chose to write consistently about the common trends in Hindu and Muslim cultures which took shape in undivided India through the centuries. Qurratul-Ain-Haider's stories continuously go back to the blessed days of Hindu-Muslim amity, when culture was not balkanised and the heart of the sup-continent was in its right place. Her 'jila watan', 'Qalander', 'Seeta Haran' and several other stories remind us again and again of the traditions of culture and thought that unite the people of the sub-continent. A host of young urdu writers also attempted to portray the class of land lords which started decaying as a result of the abolition of Zamindari system, prominent among them being Qazi Abdus Sattar, Jilami Bano, Wajida Tabassum etc. The ideological climate of India also changed with the impact of Gandhian humanistic philosophy and the concept of socialistic, democratic and secular society based on equality of opportunities and social and economic justice made the way for urdu writers to exploit the realistic vein with a quite good measure of success. Consequently they tried to weave symbols and theme upon a ground work of naturalistic detail. Ismat Chughtai wrote short stories and novels which reveal a wide range of subjects viz. sex, social problems, politics etc. In the same way Bedi presented his novel "Ek Chadar Mailee See", which is the full detail of the common folk's life in the rural Punjab. Ramanand Sagar's novel, Aur Insan Mar Gaya (And the Man Died) captivates the readers. It is a fascinating study of a sensitive soul, torn in tumult of the communal roits of 1947, and represents a firm and steady humanist approach to the mass madness of those gloomy days.

The independence brought with it not only political, but also psychological freedom to the people of India. Certain economic changes affected the family structure and women found that they were exposed to new challenges in a new society. In this new society the environment was more liberal and the opportunities it gave were infinite. It was but natural that women tried to be benefitted from this new atmosphere and the female education was encouraged. It was the pressure, both economic and social that led women to work in offices and factories. This fact contributed, as perhaps no other had, in establishing a feeling of independence in women. With these dramatic changes taking place in the society, it was difficult for women, especially in urban areas, to be guided by what their elders thought fit. Traditional feminine etiquette in the affluent segment was thrown aside and a new style of life came into being. In the nuclear family, the women had more freedom both of thought and action. Therefore break up of the joint family, increase of education and economic independence of women helped to establish the modern women. This social change has led to increase the number of women writers in urdu literature and they produced a large number of literary works which reflect the feelings and attitudes of women, especially Muslim women, on different social and domestic themes. The list of female urdu fiction writers, such as Ismat Chughtai, Qarratul Ain-Haider, Saliha Abid Hussain, Shakila Akhtar, Jilani Bano, Iffat Mohani, Hajira Nazli, Wajida Tabbasum, A.R. Khatoon, Razia Sajjad Zaheer, Azra Jamal, Nadira Khatoon, Zubaida Khatoon etc., is no less than the male writers in India.

With the development of mass communications a new change has emerged in the social and cultural scene of India during post independence period. Films and radios have been taken as the main source of enjoyment and recreation. The growing need of films and radios, among the Indian masses, has compelled the writers to compose songs and poems and to write stories, film scripts, sketches and dramas for making the programmes more attractive and appreciable. Mostly these writers produce literary works according to the prevalent taste of the mass reflecting the common socio-economic problems on the day.

After independence several urdu presses were established and a large number of books, periodicals and news papers came out. The Anjumen-i-Traqqi-e-urdu (Aligarh), the Darul-Mussanefin (Azamgarh), Nadwatul Mussanefin (Lucknow), Nasim

Book Depot (Lucknow), Maktabai-Jamia etc. catered standard works in urdu. The publications of books and pamphlets in urdu by these publishing agencies helped the urdu writers in publishing their literary works and create a market for them.

Apart from this Government of India also took initiative in developing the Indian languages including Urdu. In 1954 Sahitya Akademi was set up as a national organisation. The basic aim of this organization is to foster and to coordinate literary activities in all the Indian languages. The Akademi also arranges for the translation and publication of Indian and foreign classics into Indian languages to meet the cultural and literary needs of a multilingual society. It also makes annual awards to authors of outstanding books published in Indian languages. Many urdu writers were awarded with Sahitya Akademi awards, such as Khaja Ahmad Farooqu, Jigar Murada Badi, Akhtarul Imam, etc., for their contributions in the different forms of literature. In addition to it the Government of India also established 'Urdu Board' under the Ministry of Education to promote urdu language and literature. State governments have also established urdu Akademi tor the same purpose.

The contemporary urdu writers are quite realistic in their approaches. The never fail to voice protest against social injustice, war-mongering and economic exploitation. The attacks by China and Pakistan spurred the writers to come out with patriotic and national sentiments. Within a short time many poems, dramas, and short-stories were written on the subject and some of these appeared in book forms such as 'Cheen Chalo' by Anwar Sahiri, 'Parbat Ke Pasaban' by Raza Amrohvi, and 'Pak Zamin Napak Qadam' by Ishrat Kirat Puri. These literary works deal with the humanism, the Philosophy of war and peace and cultural values for which India stands and the trends of national integration that have emerged once again with full strength under the stress of foreign provocations.

With the increasing professionalization of literary activities in post independence era, writers find it possible and worthwhile to devote more time and effort to their writing. There is also a keener competition to get published and catch the attention of the reading public. As a result there is distinct improvement in the competence with which literature is produced. With the increasing professionalization, urdu writers are being called upon to meet the needs of the literary market. At the same time commercialization does have its unhealthy effects. It results in a lot of writing that is vulgar and debased.

C. DOMINANT THEMES (1947-1967)

The unfortunate partition of India witnessed one of the history's most passionate upheavals—terrible orgies of blood letting, looting, arson and rape—which broke the human relations and swept away the past glories of Hindu-Muslim unity. Hundreds of thousands were killed and their properties were looted and destroyed. The entire regions of Bengal, Punjab, U.P., Bihar and the North West Frontier Province were thrown into a dangerous state of communal riots. "That afternoon, in a town of East Punjab, a mob of Sikhs were reported to have seized Muslim women, stripped and raped them, and paraded them naked through the streets, some of them were slaughtered and burnt. Across the border, on the night of the 15th August, a large Muslim mob burnt down a Gradwera (Sikh temple) killing and incriminating its occupants to the number of about a score."[43] "It was impossible to count victims properly in the confussed heap of rubbles and corpses."[44] Thus the organised rioting, looting, stabbing and arson were frequent in many parts of the two countries. All classes of people joined the train of refugees. "The uprooted millions were in a terrible mental state. They had been driven from their homes under conditions of indescribable horror and misery. Not many had the time to plan their evacuation; most had to move out at the shortest possible notice. They had been

43. Hudson, H.V. : "The Great Divide : Britain-India-Pakistan". London, Hutchins, 1969, p. 403.
44. Report of the Punjab Boundry Force, by Major General T.W. Rees quoted by H.V. Hudson, p. 403.

subjected to terrible indignties, they had witnessed their houses being ransacked, looted, and set on fire by their own neighbours, they had no choice but to seek safety in flight, filled with wrath and full of anguish for numberless missing kinsmen who were still stranded in Pakistan and for their womenfolk who had been abducted."[45] The movement of refugees from and to Pakistan posed a great problem which the Central Emergency Committee had to tackle. "In the nine months between August 1947 and spring of the following year, between fourteen and sixteen million Hindus, Sikhs and Muslims were forced to leave their homes and flee to safety from blood crazed mobs. In the same period over 600,000 of them were killed."[46] According to another report "It has been estimated that up to the middle of 1948 about five and half million non-Muslims were brought across the border from West Punjab and other provinces of Western Pakistan. About the same number of Muslims moved into Pakistan from East Punjab (including the East Punjab States), Delhi, the United Provinces, Ajmer, Merwar, Alwar, Bharatpur, Gwalior and Indore. During the same period about 1.4 million non-Muslims crossed the border from East Pakistan into West Bengal. These figures do not of course take into account about 4,000,000 non-Muslims who later migrated to India from Sind."[47] Andrew Mellor also gives some statistical figure of refugees. According to his estimate, "altogether some 12,000,000 people moved between the two countries."[48]

The partition of India not only caused communal riots but also created the various socio-economic and political problems such as the problem of the division of the head-

45. Menon, V.P. : 'The Transfer of Power in India', Bombay, Orient Longmans, 1957.
46. Mosley, Leonard : "The Last days of the British Raj", New York, Harcourt, Brace and World, Inc , 1961, p. 243.
47. Menon, V.P. : 'The Transfer of Power in India, Orient Longman Private Ltd., 1957, p. 43.
48. Mellor, Andrew, "India since Partition" London, Trustile Press, 1951, p. 45.

waters; unfair division of assets; claim of refugees in regard to properties, and Kashmir—one of the most persistant of the international problems. The consequences of partition both socially and politically were much serious and of wide range and its one of the most distressing aspects, however, was the eruption of large scale Hindu-Muslim riots. According to Devanandan and Thomas even those who wanted to build a secular non communal state and society were forced to engineer with communal group interests. This was unavoidable in that state of social transition.[49]

The communal tensions are the result of the conflicts of the various social and political forces of the late 19th century such as the formations of Muslim League (1906), Hindu Mahasabha (1907), Rashtriya Swayam Sevak Sangh (1925), Jana Sangh (1951) etc. The partition of India was itself an outcome of clash and conflicts between Hindu Mahasabha and Muslim League. In 1937 Mr. V.D. Savarkar, in his presidential address of Hindu Mahasabha declared that "there are two antagonistic nations living side by side in India."[50] On that basis Mr. Jinnah framed his two-nation theory which led to the demand for the partition of the country. After the formation of Pakistan as an Islamic State, in India also the Hindu Mahasabha started to propagate an idea of "establishing Hindu Raj in Bharat with a form of Government in accordance with Hindu conceptions of polity and economy."[51] In the presidential address of 1951 Prof. Ram Singh declared that "every christian or every Muslim in India is a disruptive force."[52] Naturally these ideologies and statements given by different politicians posed and are still posing a great threat to our secular democratic society.

49. Devanandan, P.V. and Thomas, M M. Ed. 'Christian Participation Nation Building', Bangalore, National Christian Council and Christian Institute for the study of Religion and Society, 1960, p. 43.
50. Savarkar, V.P. : "Hindu Rashtra Darshan", Bombay, L.G. Khare, 1949, p. 26.
51. Election Manifesto of 1951.
52. Quoted by D.E. Smith—India—a secular state, London, Princeton University Press, 1967.

Immediately after partition the elite of Indian Muslims began to realise the blunder of the two nation theory which emerged as a great threat to their socio-economic and political integrity. "The Indian Muslims after 1947, realized that the consciousness of being a separate 'nation' could not offer any desirable solution to their problems arising out of the fear of Hindu domination."[53] As a matter of fact Maulana Azad and other nationalist Muslims tried to provide secular foundations to the politics of the Muslim community. They stressed upon the development of a democratic, non communal and secular outlook. On the other hand fanatic section among the Hindus developed a communal attitude towards Indian Muslims and treated them as 'unwilling citizens in the country.' They asked them (Indian Muslims) to go under the process of Indianization which stands for "the total rejection of everything Islamic-cum-Arab-Iranian-Turkish and acceptance of every thing, indigenous, ancient Bharatiya fine arts, mythology, heroes, festivals and even names."[54] The continuance of mistrust, suspicion and increasing communal riots created the sense of insecurity and frustration among the Indian Muslims. The psychological make up of the Muslim community thus created, pushed them to isolationism and brought them closer to the communalists.

Since 1948 the Muslim league and the Jamaat-e-Islami started to function. The attitude of these parties is community oriented. "The working of the Muslim organisations reveals certain striking common features. All the organisations are separatist and believe in maintaining a distinct political character of the community."[55]

Since 1947 India has faced various changes and challenges in the process of a newly emerging society. The achievement of independence has in same ways quickened the process of socio-economic and political changes and as such "from a

53. Shakir, Moin : "Muslims in free India', New Delhi, Kalamkar Prakashan Pvt., Ltd., 1972.
54. Ansari, Iqbal : Muslims and the National integration, Radiance, August 17, 1969, p. 4.
55. Shakir, Moin : "Muslims in Free India", p. 65.

status dominated society India is gradually emerging as an egalitarian democratic community."[56] But the process of change and progress is not very revolutionary in comparison to other developing countries. This is because of various rigid social and cultural factors on which the Indian society is based.

India's most significant but unique feature is caste system. In "It is undoubtedly an all India phenomenon in the sense that there are everywhere hereditory, endogamous groups which form a hierarchy, and that each of these of groups has a traditional association with one or two occupations. Everywhere there are brahmins, untouchables, and peasants, artisan, trading and service castes. Relations between castes are invariably expressed in terms of pollution and purity."[57] Indian social life is based on caste divisions and its loyalties are regarded as essential loyalties. Even the votes are secured and the ministries are formed on the basis of caste loyalties. "The selection of candidates, the formation of ministries and the composition of patronage dispensing committees and boards, the factor of caste is omnipresent."[58] Caste also influences the choice of the ministers regarding the appointment of the secretaries. "In the first Government of Mysore State not only were the ministers chosen on caste basis, but each had a secretary representing the minister's sub caste."[59] Caste feelings are not only prevailing in the political spheres but in day-to-day life its influences are very much significant. But inspite of its influences on the socio-economic and political structure of the Indian communities, one has to admit that a remarkable change is taking place in the rigid form of caste system, through the process of legislation and social revolution.

56. Pannikar, K.M. : "The Foundations of New India", London, George Allen & Unwin, 1963, p. 244.
57. Srinivas, M.N. : "Social Change in Modern India, Bombay, Allied Publishers, 1966, p. 3
58. Smith, D.E. : India—a secular state, London, Princeton University Press, 1967, p. 326.
59. Quoted by Charles Bettelheim : 'India Independent' English tr. by W A. Caswell, London, Macgibbon & Kee 1968, p. 42.

There are other factors such as spread of education, emergence of big cities, heavy industrialization, migration, assimilation and fusuion of culture, communication, growing feelings of nationalism and various political and economic forces, working together for the elimination of caste system both in its religious and functional aspects. The traditional social values and prejudices of close society are on the verge of decay and as such many new things are welcome and accepted in order to shape a new healthy secular and democratic society.

In the field of education, too, there has been a great change since 1947. New India has highly intelligent and sensitive young students as are to be found anywhere in the world. With a view to raise the standards of living the Government has put into operations the Five Year Plans. These Plans aim at the eradication of illiteracy and ignorance from the country. The problems of poverty and illiteracy are to some extent interdependent on each other. The standards of our people cannot be raised unless we give them education and at the same time we cannot have education unless there is economic development.[60]

An outstanding feature of educational development in the post independence era is the unprecedented rate of expansion. There has been an enormous growth in the number of educational institutions at all the different levels viz. primary, middle, secondary, collegiate, and university, and also in the volume of students.

The education of women never received so much of patronage as in the post-independent India. To-day Indian women enjoy the same status and rights as men in the society. They have been given the right to education, right to work with adequate wages and security of tenure, right to freedom of association, and right to health and leisure. With the introduction of co education a new outlook towards life has emerged. Many of our social problems and injustice are the off shoots of the irrational attitude which men and women develope towards each other. The taboo imposed by the society

60. Kirpal, Prem : A Decade of Education, Delhi, Indian Book Co., 1968, p. 28.

over the question of free mixing of the men and women cause isolation and prevent the development of proper understanding between them. It is believed that a healthy co-educational institution produces a robust outlook which in the long run helps to develop a happy family life. Young boys and girls come closer to each other as well as share common responsibilities and hence a healthy atmosphere is created for understanding each other.

After the achievement of independence the position of women, apart from education, has considerably changed. Previously a woman advocating for equality between sexes was considered aggressive and essentially non-feminine. The changes are most apparent today. "There are unmistakable sings that the traditional conceptions regarding the place and role of women are slowly changing in contemporary Indian society. The process has been generated and aided by a variety of factors which are operating almost simultaneously. Increasing opportunities for modern education, greater geographical and occupational mobility, and the emergence of new economic patterns are in the main responsible for this trend."[61] The opening up of opportunities for women has been accelerated in the last two decades. It can not, however, be denied that though theoretically the equality of women has been recognised but the older attitudes are not dead. The middle class, both in urban and rural sectors, are often considered as the sentinel of old ideas. The forces of modernisation, which have started operating in our society, are slowly but steadily breaking the hard core of conservatism. Increasing number of families in this class are now developing modern outlook. As a result, these days we find a large number of women students in educational institution and a majority of them belong to middle class families. Higher education of girls is no more considered as unwanted or unethical rather it is taken as necessary and beneficial. The parents seldom feel hesitation to

61. Dube, S.C. : Men's and women's role in India—a sociological review, taken from "women in the new Asia", ed. by. Barbara E. Ward Paris, UNESCO, 1965, p. 202.

send their daughter to coeducational institutions and also do not mind for their participation in campus activities.

The changing economic set up, the growing standard of living and also the inflation can be held as contributory factors in the change of outlook towards the role of women in society. 130th men and women of India have begun to realize that the supreme goal of women's life is not circumscribed to merely love making, dutifulness to husband, bearing and domestic work. They have begun to realize that women's life has a higher and a more serious objecrive."[62]

Indian constitution also guarantees the equality of sex. The right to equality has clearly been described in the clauses 14 and 15 of the Indian constitution. "The state shall not deny to any person equality before the law or the equal protection of the law within the territory of India. The state shall not discriminate against any citizen on grounds of religion, race, caste, sex, place of birth or any of them... No citizen shall on grounds only of religion, race, caste, sex, place of birth or any of them, be subjected to any disability, liability restriction or condition with regard to access to public places, or the use of public wells, tanks"[63] etc.

Several Legislations have also been enacted in the post independence era, with a view to elevate the status and position of women in society. The significant among them are Hindu Marriage Act of 1955,[64] Hindu succession Act of 1956,[65] Special Marriage Act[66], and Dowry Prohibition Act of 1961.[67]

Since the attainment of independence women have been given some high administrative and diplomatic positions in the country. "Indian women are also beginning to make their influence in world affairs. Their appearance at international

62. Desai quoted by Promilla Kapur : "Marriage and the working women in India", Delhi, Vikas Publications, 1970, pp. 4-5.
63. Ibid.
64. Thomas, P. : Indian women through the ages, Bombay, Asia Publishing House, 1964, p. 365.
65. Ibid.
66. Ibid., p. 368.
67. Ibid., p. 370.

conferences is no longer greeted with surprised congratulations that they should be there at all and able to apeak English so fluently."[68] We have had a galaxy of beauty and brains both in parliament and government.[69]

India is essentially an agricultural country. Thus the changes which have taken place since independence stem in part from the agrarian reforms, modifying legal ties and property ties. "The land with its resources and the means of production as well as the means of distribution and exchanging should belong to the community and be administered in its own interest."[70] Hence after the attainment of freedom India has made significant transformation in the agrarian economy by abolising Zamindari system, traditional system of land Tenure prevailing in India. Zamindari system was largely responsible for the continuously deteriorating conditions of tenant farmers. The Zamindars not only derived large incomes without in any way contribution to production but also possessed immense power over the tenants and even more over the agricultural labourers which they exercised, as a rule, in an inhuman manner. "But by the end of March, 1966 the allocation of intermediaries was fully implemented, in M.P.; Punjab, Assam, Gujrat, Madras, Maharashtra, Rajasthan, Andhra, U.P., Orissa, West Bengal, Bihar and Kerala."[71]

Apart from the specific affirmation of socialist pattern of society as our goal since 1954, by the congress and the Government, efforts have been made for the establishment of classless society, the reduction of inequalities, prevention of concentration of economic power or its mitigation where it does exist,

68. O'Mally, L.S.S. : Modern India and the West, Oxford University Press, London, 1941, p. 477.
69. Article entitled, "Women in politics" by Amita Mallik in Sunday Hindustan Standard Colour Magazine dated 29-7-'73, Calcutta, p. 6-7.
70. Quoted by H.D. Malaviya : "Land reforms in India", New Delhi, 1955, p. 79.
71. Ghosh, Alak : Indian Economy : Its nature and problems. Calcutta World Press, Pvt. Ltd., 1968, p. 231.

social security against the risks of sickness, unemployment and death, payment of minimum and living wages, promotion of justice—social, political and economic, ceiling on personal income, land to the tiller and, therefore, abolition of rentiers, i.e. all agricultural incomes derived from property without personal labour, public ownership of all key industries and increasing importance of public sector in all industries, promotion of decentralized industrial sector and its progressive cooperativization, occupation of all strategic points in the economy by the state and steering the later in the direction of a socialist society, building up a cooperative structure in rural economy for credit, cultivation, marketing, crop planning and essential services, and so on. The planning commission was appointed in 1950 in order to make an assessment of the existing human, capital and material resources of the community and to formulate plans for the balanced utilisation of existing as well as potential resources. As a matter of fact Five Year Plans were introduced to bring planned economic revolution in the country.

After the independence India has made much progress in urbanization. The cities and larger towns have grown more rapidly and the rates of growth are significant because they have provided one of the important environmental pre-conditions for modernization of Indian society. In the words of Pitambar Pant, 'Urbanization is an important aspect of the process of economic and social change in India..."[72] Urbanization is not an isolated factor. It is accompanied by increasing industrialization, technological progress, and also several other factors such as quicker means of transport and communication, population growth, improvement in agricultural techniques etc.

Ever since 1947 India has made significant progress in the field of mass media of communication. The mass media of communication are very much effective in causing social transformations. "The important thing is that a certain level

72. "India's urban future" Ed. by Roy Turner, Bombay, Oxford University Press, 1962, p. 182.

and stage of communication development have to accompany a certain stage and level of social development generally. Without a sophisticated and efficient development of communication, the base of population, cooperation, industrialization, education and skills needed in modern industrial society can not possibly be established."[73]

Though the effectiveness of the mass media communication is yet to reach a large section of the people living in the remote parts of the country it has influenced our social life in several other ways. It has broadened, as pointed cut earlier, our outlook. The limited and parachoial nature of our outlook of the past is being replaced by the one which is definitely more liberal and international in character. We are now in a position to weigh ourselves politically, socially, culturally and ethically with other nations and to understand in some cases our deficiencies as compared to the developed nations.

Basically India lives in villages. The rural development programmes in India are rapidly changing the landscape in countryside and generating a sense of optimism regarding future among the village folk. The most striking step taken towards rural upliftment is known as the community development programme which was initiated in 1952.[74] The Community Development movement was conceived from the beginning as one touching on all aspects of rural life. An important aspects of the community development programme is the Panchayati Raj which has been thought necessary to decentralize and democratize administration of community development. The system constitutes a far reaching change in the structure of local administration and rural development.

Indian constitution guarantees the establishment of universal adult suffrage, and as a matter of fact multiparty system has developed in India. Political parties are the

73. Schramm, Wilbur : "Mass Media and National Development", Stanford, Stanford University Press, 1964, p. 41.

74. Mukerji, B. : 'Objectives and methods of Community Development' taken from 'Extension Education in Community Development, New Delhi, Directorate of Extension, Ministry of Food and Agriculture, Government of India, 1961, p. 49.

essential phenomena of a democratic government. They play an important role of mobilizing the electorates and in this process the common people develop political awareness as well as they become a functional part of the participant society. These parties have been very much helpful to the Indian citizens in fostering political attitudes and sensitiveness both in rural and urban areas.

In the fields of science and technology also tremendous changes have occurred and as such India has entered into a new phase of technological advancement with the comprehensive development programme, such as, constructions of high power dams and high ways, rapid industrialization, mechanization of agriculture, production of aircrafts, ships, diesel engines and rise in the standard of living.

Since 1947, the most significant facet of Indian foreign policy has been its firm belief in non-alignment. India has chosen the road of political democracy and tried to maintain peace in the sub-continent. As a matter of fact, in 1954, Pandit Jawaharlal Nehru, the then Prime Minister of India, evolved the five principles of international relation (Panchsheel) and incoroprated them in the treaty he signed with China.[75]

In 1959 China, however, accupied Tibet and invaded India's frontiers in 1962. It was a crucial year for India. The news of the invasion created unprecedented sense of unity in the country. It rose as one man to help and repel aggression. In a moment, all differences-political, social, religious, linguistic and regional-were forgotten and everybody became animated by the one common desire of defending the country and resisting the invasion. The invasion produced complete unity throughout the country.

75. Panchsheel :—(i) Mutual respect for each other's territorial integrity and sovereignty (ii) Non aggression (iii) Non-interference in each other internal affairs (iv) Equality and mututal benefit and (v) Peaceful co-existence.

Quoted from "My years with Nehru : The Chinese Betrayal" by B.N. Mallik, Bombay, Allied Publishers; 1971, p. 151.

After the Sino-Indian conflict India was again attacked by Pakistan in 1965. China wanted to fish in the troubled waters by demanding the withdrawal of some of our installations from the borders of Sikkim and Tibet. Consequently, firm action was taken by the security council of the United Nations and there was a ceasefire which both combatants complied. In January 1966, the President of Pakistan and Lal Bahadur Shastri, the then Prime Minister of India, went to the Soviet City of Tashkent and signed an agreement for complete withdrawal of forces behind their respective borders to the 1949 ceasefire line.[76] The withdrawal was affected but the cause of the disputes remained.

Thus between the years 1947 of 1967 India has faced the various changes and challenges in the process of a newly emerging society. India has not only fought with Pakistan and China but she had to combat with other problems inside the country e.g. Language problem, unemployment problem, population problem etc.

Finally, it can be said that independence of the country could not produce much of enthusiasm in the minds of the Indian Muslims. They had to face the hardship and miseries which followed the division of the country. Socially also the Muslims of India were divided into three groups viz. Indian Muslims, Punjabi Muslims or the Muslims of West Pakistan and the Muslims of East Bengal. In short they lost their homogeneity. Politically, the Indian Muslims developed a sense of frustration and considered themselves as being treated like second class citizen. The Muslim political parties automaticallv became defunct and they sought the protection of the major political party of the country viz. Indian National Congress. Economically the Position of the Indian Muslims was no better. The protection provided to them by the British authorities was withdrawn and the end of faudalism which followed the independence dealt severe blows to the economic condition of the Indian Muslims.

76. Saxena, K.C. : Pakistan—Her Relation with India (1947-67) New Delhi, Vir Publishing House, 1966, p. 205.

The dominant themes, described above, also affected the subject and content of the urdu novels during the period. The analysis of the novels in the following pages of the present thesis will reveal the impact of these dominant themes on urdu novels and also the manners in which the urdu novelists have tried to find out solutions of the problems faced by the general mass including Muslim community of India.

2

Methodology

It is unfortunate that the sociological study of literature has not yet become systematic. The volume of work done so far is not significant. They are scattered and no attempt has yet been made for any co-ordination. The different authors also vary widely on the basis of their approaches. Literature, of course, has long been recognized as a product of the social situation and the early attempts to analyse it was mainly philosophical in nature. Till that period sociology also could not gain the status of an empirical science. The idea of Marx and Engels viz. economic determinism of literature, failed to establish a satisfactory relationship between the two. Toynbee claimed literature as the integral part of culture. Sorokin is also of this opinion. But inspite of all these attempts no significant achievement is marked and a comprehensive sociology of literature has not been written.

The absence of a quantitative method makes the sociological study of literature obviously difficult. The quantitative methods and statistics are considered as legitimate tools of sociology at present. Since Pareto's idea of logico-experimental method and scientific sociology appeared, the trend has gone in favour of empirical investigation. The behaviouristic and metaphysical approaches have now become obsolete. "It is not correct to think that the quantitative method can not be applied to the study of the relationship between society and literature, Sorokin's use of quantitative method, however primitive they might be, can be made refined. Another possibility is to study the number of registered borrowers in the public libraries in a city and to compare them with the total population. From such studies we can arrive at the conclusion about the response which a particular writer getts."[1]

Several studies have been made of the relations between the literature and society that involve the use of quantitative techniques. But Inglis has tried to find out the temporal priority of social as against literary influences by analysing the pattern of economic and occupational attributes of the heroines of popular fictions. She studied several hundred items of fictions that appeared in a leading 'mass' magazine over a 35 year period and compared the pattern revealed in these sources with changes in the same attributes of American women of similar age as set forth in the census data. According to her, "the functional trend (attributes) lags about a decade behind the actual trend.[2] This study supports the thesis that literature, at least of the 'mass' type reflects social changes rather than causes them by inducing readers to imitate characters in fiction.

In 1946 Bernard Berleson and Patricia Salter analysed about 200 short stories published in eight 'mass media' magazines in two years and found that fictional portrayals of 'minority group' members are consistently less favourable than portrayals of 'majority' American i.e. those who are white, protestant, English speaking, and of Anglo-saxon ancestry.[3]

M.C. Albrecht, in an interesting paper has attempted to test the hypothesis that literature reflects cultural values—specially the values of the family. A group of 153 short stories selected from magazines that were classified on the basis of certain technical criteria as representing different cultural levels, was studied for themes expressing adherence to or rejection of the values set forth in the configuration. He

1. Biswas, D.K. : Sociology of Major Bengali Novels, the Academic Press, Gurgaon, 1974, p. 21.
2. Inglis, R. : "An objective approach to the relationship between fiction and society" : American Sociological Review, 3.4 (1938), p. 630.
3. Berelson, Bernard and Salter, Patricia : "Minority and Majority Americans : An Analysis of Magazine Fiction", Public Opinion Quarterly, 10 (1946) pp. 168-90.

worked out the percentage of adherence to or rejection of the configuration of family values appearing in the short stories and discovered different patterns according to cultural values.[4]

In 1948 divorce and prejudice in fiction was studied by Bernett and Guren. They attempted to determine agreement between literacy content and statistical data on occupation and population distribution in the United States. The results have pointed to an emphasis on wide spread American attitude and ideas, reinforcing the idea that literature reflects common cultural values.[5]

A recent and most stimulating contribution to the sociological study of literature is Lowenthal's, 'Literature and the image of man'. This book presents a sociological analysis and interpretation of selected novels and dramas written by European authors between 1600 and 1960, including works by several prominent Spanish and French writers, only play by Shakespear, two novels by Goethe, several plays of Ibsen, and the novels of Hamsun. Lowenthal's main thesis is that creative writers through their selection—often unconscious—of plots, characterization, depiction of milieus, and emphasis on values, convincingly portray man's relation to his society and times.[6]

CONTENT ANALYSIS—AS A TOOL OF SOCIAL RESEARCH

The method of content analysis is recent years, is getting increasing attention. It is a research method, developed in the last few decades, for investigating a broad spectrum of problems which the content of communication serves as the basis of inference. It is useful whenever the problem requires precise and replicable methods for analyzing those

4. Albrecht, M.C. : Does Literature Reflect Common Values ? American Sociological Review, 21, (1956) pp. 22-29.
5. Bernett, J.H. and Guren, R. : "Recent American Divorce Novels, 1938-1945' : Social Forces, 26 (1948), pp. 332-37.
6. Lowenthal, Leo. : Literature and the image of man; Beacon Press, 1951.

aspects of symbolic behaviour which may escape casual scrutiny. In other words content analysis is likely to prove especially useful for atleast three general class of research problems.

Firstly, content analysis may be helpful from technical point of view, when the volume of material to be examined is such that the investigator must either:

(i) continue his study to some sample of the total universe of communication
(ii) use a team of assistants each with his own subjective predispositions, or
(iii) both.

Secondly, content analysis as a tool of research enables an investigator to study about the persons or situations which no longer exist and can be ascertained only by analyzing the contents of the communications belonging to that period or those persons. Thus it serves as a 'last resort' approach to social research when more direct techniques of analysis are ruled out by circumstances.

Thirdly, the most frequent application of content analysis has been for the purpose of describing the attributes of the message. There is a general criticism that it lacks quantitative approach, but George is of this view that "qualitative analysis of a limited number of crucial communications may often yield better clues to the particular intentions of a particular speaker at one moment in time than more standardized techniques."[7] Pools also explains this point: "It should not be assumed that qualitative methods are insightful and quantitative ones merely mechanical methods for checking hypothesis. The relationship is a circular one, each provides new insight on which the other can feed."[8]

The effectiveness of content analysis as a tool of sociological researches can further be explained by mentioning the different

7. George, A.L. : 'Quantitative and qualitative approaches to content analysis' In I de. S. 1959, p. 7.
8. Pool, I. de S. (Ed.) 'Trends in content analysis' Urbana : University of Illinois Press, 1959, p. 192.

types of problems which can be studied with the help of this method. The important among them as mentioned by Ole R. Holsti,[9] are as follows:

(a) What differences among cultures are reflected in the songs and literature of various nations (Sebald, 1962; Lewin, 1947) ?
(b) To what extent have the political symbols of the New Deal been adopted by American conservatives (Prothro, 1956) ?
(c) What differences characterize the language behaviour of Schizophrenic and normal persons (Mann, 1944; Fair banks, 1944) ?
(d) Is editorial support of a political candidate also reflected in biased news sections (Kobre, 1953; Klein and Maccoby, 1954) ?
(e) What has been the Soviet reaction to Voice of American broadcasts (InKeles, 1952) ?
(f) Is the Riesman hypothesis about the increasing other-directedness of American Society supported by changing content of consumer goods advertising (Dornbusch and Hickman, 1959) ?
(g) How is sentence length related to the comprehensibility of literature (Coleman 1962) ?

Barelson defines the method of content analysis as "a research technique for the objective, systematic and quantitative description of the manifest content of communication."[10]

I.L. Jains defines the method of content analysis, "as refering to any technique:

(a) for the classification of the sign—vehicles,
(b) which relies solely upon the judgements (which theoretically, may range from perceptual discriminations to sheer guesses) of an analyst or groups of

9. Holsti, Ole R. : "Content Analysis" In Hand Book of Social Psychology. Edited by Grader Lindzey and Eliot Aronson. California, Addison, 1968, p. 601-02.

10. Sellitz, C., Jahods, M., Cook M.S. : Research Methods in Social Relations, Henry Holt, New York, 1959, p. 335.

analysts as to which sign-vehicles fall into which categories,

(c) on the basis of explicitly formulated rules,

(d) provided that analysts judgement is regarded as the reports of a scientific observer."[11]

According to Barcus, 'the term content analysis is used here to mean the scientific analysis of communications messages . . . The method is broadly speaking the 'scientific method' and while being Catholic in nature, it requires that analysis be rigorous and systematic."[12]

In the opinion of Stone, "contant analysis refers to any procedure for assessing the relative extent to which special references, attitudes or themes permeate a given message or document."[13]

Cartwright says, "we propose to use the terms 'content analysis' and 'coding' inter-changeably to refer to the objective, systematic and quantitative description of any symbolic behaviour."[14]

From the definitions given above it appears that like all other methods of scientific research the method of content analysis also possesses the qualities of objectivity, systematic treatment of the data and finally generalization. Thus we can say that the term content analysis can be regarded as the application of the principles of scientific research to the

11. Janis, I.L. "The problem of validating content analysis" In the language of politics : Studies in quantitative Semantice Ed. by H.D. Lasswell and N. Leites et. al. New York, George Steward, 1949, p 55.
12. Barcus, F E. quoted by Ole R. Holsti "Content Analysis" In "Hand Book of Social Psychology" ed by Grander Lindzey and Elliot Aronson. California, Addison, 1968.
13. Stone, P.J. : An introduction to the General Inquirer : a computer system for the study of spoken or written material, Harvard University, 1964.
14. Cartwright, D.P. : 'Analysis of qualitative material ! In Research Methods in the Behavioural Sciences, Edited by L. Festinger and D. Katz. New York, Holt, Rinehart and Winston, 1953. p. 4242.

analysis of communication content. In sociological researches the problem of analysing qualitative material is often faced. The social scientists want to classify the content of qualitative materials into appropriate categories so that it can be described in an orderly way. "This process of classification into categories is commonly known as 'content analysis' or 'coding'. The former term is more frequently used in reference to qualitative materials recorded from nature; the later is more commonly employed in the analysis of materials created by the research."[15]

The present study as the title suggests, attempts to investigate into the social and cultural background of major Urdu novels. Specifically speaking it is a study of the relationship between society and its literature which is the subject matter of that branch of the science of society called as sociology of literature. In this study the attention has particularly, been focused on investigation of the representative character of the Urdu novels. In other words, the interest is focused on the enquiry, aimed at finding out whether and in what manner and extent the Urdu novels have reflected the trends of their contemporary social order. The hypothesis, in brief, is that literature is a mirror of the society. It is the 'representation of life through the medium for social creation viz., language, and 'a vital record of what men have seen in the life, and thought and felt about it'. Literature, in other words, is a 'social document faithfully recording the features of the time'. It is like a recorded history of the period of its composition.

Berelson has mentioned three approaches to the analysis of symbolic materials. "In the first, the researcher is interested primarily in the characteristics of the content itself. In the second, he tries to make valid inferences from the nature of the content to characteristics of the producers of the content or its causes. In the third he interprets the content as to reveal something about the nature of its audience or its

15. Festinger. L and Katz, D. ; Research Methods in the Behavioural Sciences, American Publishing Co. (P) Ltd., 1953.

effects. Any single study may not adopt more than one of these approaches.[16]

In the present study the first approach only has been adopted. As suggested by Berelson, 'Interest in the first approach will lead one to focus either on the substantive nature or upon the form of the content."[17]

An attempt has been made, in the present study, to analyse the social situations as depicted in the mojor Urdu novels published during 1947-1967 and find out to what extent they are true representations of the dominant socio-cultural themes of the period. The descriptions of 'Dominant socio-cultural Themes, and evolution of Urdu literature have been added with a view to provide a background which helps to ascertain the representative character of the novels. The method applied here can be called as historical, which is essentially descriptive. But as claimed by Lundberg, "even strictly historical method, however, tends to merge gradually and more or less objectively into the methods of natural science. To the extent that historians go beyond the nature mere recording to facts in their temporal sequence, and become 'comparative historians' that is, attempt to reduce their data to types, and to generalize from them, history becomes a natural science."[18]

The study among other things, has also attempted to assess the impact of modern western systems viz. Marxism and Freudianism. This has been done by applying the method of content analysis. The tables which have been used for the content analysis are constructed on the basis of the model suggested by Berelson.

The novels, for the purpose of analysis, have been selected on the basis of random sampling. At the first step the authors were selected from a list of eminent Urdu novelists and secondly the selection of their novels were done from the list of major novels written by respective novelists. The sample was drawn with the help of Tippett tables which are generally

16. Ibid.
17. Ibid.
18. Lundberg, G.A. : Social Research—A study in Methods of Gathering Data, Longmans, Green & Co. New York, 1942, p. 114.

applicable, though some limitations to their use have been described by Yule and Kendall and Babington-Smith. "A random sample is one which is so drawn that the researcher, from all pertinent points of view, has no reason to believe a bias will result. In other words, the units of the universe must be so arranged that the selection process gives equiprobability of selection to every unit in that universe."[19] The term 'major' has been used to denote the novels which became popular during this period.

At this point a question may be asked about the justification of selecting only one novel for each novelist. This has been done on the assumption that any one popular novel of a particular novelist reveals his angle of vision, personality as well as the impact of social order upon him. Generally, the novelists are calssified according to the content of their writings. Each novelist is, by himself, a type and often belongs to one or the other category of writers. In other words each novelist has his special feature even though, in a broad spectrum, he can be identified with a particular group based either on ideology, style, region, or content etc. The novels written by a particular novelist are not unrelated fragments. They exibit continuity and develop a unique pattern which exposes the personality of the writer. Selection of only one novel for each novelist, therefore, does not make the study unrealistic. The limitation of space, at the same time, does not permit inclusion of all the works of a particular novelist or more than one of his popular novels in the study.

Another question which can be raised as to why the researcher decides to change the authors and the novels for content analysis in chapters 5 and 6 respectively ? Why not the same novels, as discussed in chapter 7, were taken into consideration? The position, however, can be explained by pointing out the fact that unlike chapter 4 the novels selected for the content analysis in chapters 5 and 6 are the two schools or groups of novelists which developed under the

19. Goode, W.J. & Hatt, P.K. : Methods in Social Research, McGraw-Hill Co. Inc., New York, 1952, p. 214.

influence of two very significant ideas viz. Marxism and Freudianism which were imported to this country from the West. In chapter 4 the content of the novels selected for analysis were of general nature. In other words by analyzing the content of the novels mentioned in chapter 4 the researcher attempts to establish the hypothesIs which has been persented in the chapter entitled, sociology of literature. The analysis presented in the subsequent chapters namely 5 and 6 makes the study more focused in nature. Two specific trends of the society have been taken and by analysing the content of the novels it has been proved that these novels bear the influences of those trends. Such focused approach makes the thesis, probably, more sound methodologically.

As regards the changes made in the authors and the novels it can be justified on the ground that all the writers or novelists were not necessarily influenced either by Marxism or Freudianism. At no stage of literary development such homogeneity can be expected. This reminds one of the concept of society as a prism. The trends are many and the different groups are influenced in different manners and intensity by these trends. This factor leads to the formation of different groups of writers in a particular literature. This, however, is not unique for any particular language. To take the instance of Bengali novelists one finds the two groups of novelist influenced by the Marxism and Freudian concepts respectively emerged during the post world war I period. "The scientific analysis of class struggle by Karl Marx brought a revolution in the realm of thought. When it was reflected in the Bengali novels of the post World War I period, the entire literary measures were revolutionised and the modern progressive literature started from this point—Marx based his ideas on material and historical dialectic and his ideas were accepted by the Bengali novelists."[20]

The psycho-analytical trends which developed in the contemporary European literature as a result of World War I also remarkably influenced the Bengali literature. This age

20. Biswas, D.K. : Op cit, p. 157.

of ultra-realism has been named as 'Kallol Yug' in Bengali literature. The writers of this age ignored the moral orientation of the social mind attempted to develop the literature based on normally acceptable sex centred life. In other words the main source of inspiration of these writers was basically instinctive and the sexual relationship between man and woman was undoubtedly the subject matter of their novels."[21]

The Urdu novelists also were influenced by the ideas of Marx and Freud. They can be categorised in two distinct groups. Hence for the purpose of content analysis the selection of authors and their novels have been done from these two groups respectively.

21. Ibid., p. 182.

3

Evolution of Urdu Novel

Novel is at present time universally recognised as one of the most popular forms of literary art. Its resources and capacities appear to be commensurate with the realities and consciousness of the modern epoch. It is broadening, growing, beginning to be serious, impossioned, living form of literary study and social research.

The novel as a new form of literature developed under the influence of capitalist society. Capitalism brought a great deal of changes in the socio-economic structure of the society. The most important phenomenon of the capitalist society, however, was the emergence of middle class. This newly created class of people was the real patrons of novel as both the readers and writers of novels came from this stratum of the society. Therefore, novel can be described as a new invention in the field of literature and not simply the successor of ballad, epic or romance. It emerged as an expression of the new social mind. "We can even say that not only is the novel the most typical creation of the bourgeois literature, it is also its great creation. It is a new form. It did not exist, except in very rudimentary form, before that modern civilization which began with the Renaissance and like every new art it has served its purpose of extending and deepening human consciousness."[1]

The spread of urban civilization has paved the way for the enlargement of middle class. There was a marked rise in the

1. Fox, Ralph : "The Novel and the People". Moscow, Foreign Language Publishing House, 1964, p. 80.

number and riches of the shopkeepers, independent tradesmen as well as administrative and clerical employees in the society. These growing urban middle classes started prose narrative technique and preferred it over the poetry for the expression of their ideas. Earlier poetry was the dominant medium of expression of thoughts and emotions. But this traditional decorum of literary form was replaced by an easy and loose form of literature viz. novel which allows a more immediate imitation of individual experience set in its temporal and spatial environment than do other literary forms. The majority of readers in the last two hundred years have found in the novel the literary form which most closely satisfied their wishes for a close correspondence between life and art.

The scientific and technological advancement brought a great change in the reading world. Especially the invention of printing press made possible for the easy publication of books, journals, magazines, and newspapers which enlarged the scope of literature and ultimately cleared the way for the popularity of novels among the reading mass.

The gradual extension of the literary and the reading public also affected the development of this new form of literature. The extension of literacy has been increasingly tempting the writers of fiction with the prospect of wider horizon and bigger audiences, on the other hand proliferation of specialised interests—national and international politics, crime and detection, espionage and counter espionage, sport and pastime, monopoly and big business, class-war and the horror of thermo-nuclear war, airtravel and the possibility of space travel —has led to the 'Specialist novels'. These novels, with different themes, explore the problems of contemporary civilization and deal with the world of human feelings and thought with breadth and penetration.

Libraries have also played an important role in the rise of novels. Most circulating libraries stocked with all types of novels led to the most notable increase in the reading public for fiction. It can be very well observed that the majority of the reading public of the libraries are potential novel readers. Particulrly, women of the upper and middle classes have been largely composed of potential novel readers as it was not usual for them to engage in politics, business, or the administration. Such women, therefore, have a great deal of Leisure and this leisure is often spent by omnivorous reading.

The development of capitalism is associated with the idea of individual freedom within the society. Capitalism prepared the way for the rapid increase of economic specialization which, combined with a less rigid homogeneous social structure and more democratic political system, enormously increased the sense of individual freedom. It is generally accepted that the modern society is based on the concept of individualism. The existence of such a society depends on a particular type of socio-economic and political organization which provides its members an autonomy irrespective of any social discrimination. As a matter of fact the capitalism brought changes in the socio-economic and political structure of the society i.e., the emergence of industrial capitalism and the growth of 'industrial-urban' culture etc. This new social order rejected the traditional standard of ethics and caused the decline of the religious forces. Outlook of the people changed with simulteneous advancement of science and technology. They became more and more rational in their ideas. The novelists also observed those changes and reflected them in the domain of literature. They expressed the diverse elements of individualism more completely than the previous writers.

The concept of individualism also brought changes in the social status of women. It is true that the idea of freedom of women has until recently been the exception rather than the rule in the history of human society. The position of women was not satisfactory and rather disadvantageous. The emergence of a new social order, under the influence of individualism, changed the inferior social position of women and number of restrictions on their movements were withdrawn in accordance with the temperament of the age. Naturally, the changing status and position of women in the society also became the theme of the fiction. Novelists took up their cause and laid emphasis on several problems relating to the women viz. their unsatisfactory status, the dowry system, the implication of marriage by choice, illegitimate sexual union, right to divorce, the romantic relationships etc.

Novel is, therefore, a legitimate subject of sociological investigation. It is a cultural phenomenon which reflects past interaction as interpreted by the author and influences subsequent interaction on the part of the reader. It is a 'living source book' to which we go for insights into important sociological concerns such as the group, the social self, social class, social mobility, social change and social institutions. These informations are regarded valid and subject to investigations by many sociologists of our time.

The world 'novel' has been derived from the Latin adjective 'novellus' diminutive of 'novus', meaning new. When applied to fiction it means a new tale or story. It was adopted in the sixteenth century by the English language through an Italian word 'novella', used to describe a short tale portraying the incidents of everyday living.[2] Hence, novel is that type of prose fiction which is written as a serious imitation of reality. It observes the probabilities of actual existence in its use of plot and action and its depiction of character...the novel portrays the most intimate aspects of private life, and it can also depict a large social group without losing sight of the gesture and attitude that characterize individuals within the group."[3]

Novel is the logical literary vehicle of culture as it is concerned with man, nature, real life and manners. It is, infact, a pseudo-scientific social documentation. It explores the inter-relations between man and nature, between individual man and collective man (or the social aggregate). The greater novelists have tried to hold the mirror up to the life of their times. According to Ian Watt "The novel is a full and authentic report of human experience, and is therefore under an obligation to satisfy its reader with such details of the story as the individuality of the actors concerned, the particulars of the times and places of their actions. . . . . . ."[4].

2. Encyclopedia Americana, New York, Americana Corporation, 1966, V. 2, p. 510 f.

3. Ibid : p. 510 g.

4. Watt, Ian : Op. cit., p. 33.

Novel is distinguished from other genres and from previous forms of fiction by the amount of attention it habitually accords both to the individualization of its characters and to the detailed authentic presentation of their environments." "The novelist studies men and women; he is concerned with their actions and their thoughts, their errors and their meanness; the countless forms of beauty and constantly varying moods to be seen among them, the forces which act upon them; the passions, prejudices, hopes, and fears which pull them this way and that."[5]

A writer of real creative genius takes only those events and incidents which have come within the range of his own experience and observation. He analysis and presents an exact picture of the social surroundings of the age in which he lives. Premchand, an eminant urdu novelist, for example, has portrayed the Indian rural life and its problems such as the caste differences, orthodox religious practices, the sexual life etc. with appreciable accuracy. In the same way Krishan Chandar's novels reveal a deep sense of economic and social awareness of the changing Indian society. The novelists not only reflect the picture of external aspects of the age but they also focus on its underlying truth. "The contemporary novels are the mirror of the age but a very special kind of mirror, a mirror that reflects not merely the external features of the age, but also its inner face, its nervous system, the coursing of its blood and unconscious promptings and conflicts which sway it."[6] In our daily experiences we are lost in the largeness of all around us. We can not understand all that is going on. But a good novel catches a part of what is going on and holds it for us, and we can see relationships, of actual time and events. Thus the aim of the novelist is to come as near as possible to the reality of human life. The modern reader has also become more subtle. He no longer goes to the novel just to amuse himself or to

5. Besant. Walter : "The art of fiction", 'The Art of the Essay, Ed. by Leslie Fielder.
6. Allen, Walter, "Reading A Novel", London, Phonix House, 1949, p. 14.

'escape' but to find the inner meaning of life. He wants from the novelist not only an outside photograph but a portrait of the whole man.

The origin of novel in Urdu literature can be traced with the Fort William College which was founded under the guidance of Dr. John Gilchrist at Calcutta by the end of the 18th century. The object of this college was only to teach Indian languages to young English officers with other subjects viz. Law, ethics, Jurisprudence, science, etc., because it was highly necessary for them to have their men trained in the language of the country for administrative reasons. In order to achieve this objective the college had to undertake the compilation of works in different subjects in the different languages and hence a large number of Hindustani (Urdu) scholars and writers were employed to work under the guidance of Gilchrist who himself was a good scholar of Hindustani, Persian and Arabic. A large number of stories were translated into Urdu from Sanskrit and Persian such as Mir Amman's 'Bagh-o-Bahar' (Garden and Spring), Syed Haider Buksh's 'Tota Kahani' (The tales of a Parrot), and 'Araish-i-Mahfil' (Ornament of the assembly) etc. With the publication of these stories at the 'Fort William College Press' a new appetite for stories developed in the society. Consequently, a large number of writers began to write and translate many intersting stories which ultimately could create an atmosphere for the rise of Urdu novel. These stories were mostly supernatural, adventurous and stereotyped and dealt "mainly with adventures of Lovers, the magic of enchanters and wizards, the fights of princes with Sorcerors and sudden metamorphosis of men into animals."[7] But from sociological point of view these stories are very important because they give not only the picture of the contemporary society but also reveal the social and cultural awareness of the age. Though the characters are mainly of Gaints, Witchmen, Princess and Fairies but, to some extent, their joys, sorrows, customs, habits and experiences are described in the social environment of that time. These stories

7. Saksena, Ram Babu, "History of Urdu Literature" p. 318. Ram Narain Lal Allahabad, 1927.

were written at the time when Indian society, particularly Muslim society, was facing socio-economic and political unrest and chaos posed by the rising of the British power and the fall of the Mughal Empire. Nawabs and Jagirdars were under the protection of the British Government, and some of them were confined within their palaces. Common people were neglected on the various social and economic fronts. As a matter of fact the glories of the past and the precarious conditions of the present created a deep sense of inferiority and frustration which compelled them to invent pastimes. They invented different types of games, composed poems with colourful themes and wrote enchanting stories to forget the present like an Ostrich who covers face in the desert to escape from the enemy. These stories, technically, can not be categorised as novels but they prepared the stage for the rise of novel.

With the establishment of urdu press at Lucknow, Kanpur, and Delhi new demand for urdu fictions lincreased. In 1858 the urdu press was started by Munshi Nawal Kishore at Lucknow. This press played an important role in the development of urdu language and literature. In 1859 this press started a newspaper—'Audh Akhbar' which was instrumental in bringing some eminent fiction writers like Maulana Abdul Heleem Sharar, Pandit Ratannath Sarshar, and Shaukat Thanvi to lime light. One of the greatest achievements of this press in the field of fiction was to create an interest for urdu fictions by publishing stories translated from Arabic, Persian and Sanskrit.

The urdu novels, in true sense, were written during the end of the 19th century when sir Syed Ahmad Khan started his reformative activities to improve the socio-economic and intellectual standards of Muslims in India. He had inaugurated an era of revolutionary changes in Muslims thought by introducing a scheme of Muslim education. The scheme had a tremendous impact no the life and thought of the Muslim community. As a matter of fact it acted as renaissance which had shaken the traditional values and lit a new candle of hope in the hearts of Muslim intelligentia who came forward and took up the task of reformation. The middle class, on the other hand, was growing up in new economic and intellectual environment. The younger generations within this class were increasingly taking English education and new ideas were fast pouring into their minds. New sentiments which were unknown earlier began to germinate and hence the ways of orthodox thinking and feeling began to wither away. The influence of the two—the new ways of living and new education—started modernising the middle class society. Thus the society that emerged after the holocaust of 1857 witnessed the disappearance of the remnants of Mughal aristocracy, the establishment of modern administration, the spread of new ideas and new education. All these factors caused transformation of the social milieu of northern provinces. Thus under the stress of the changed atmosphere urdu novel began to develop by migrating from the traditional romanticism of Dastan to realism. This age of novel writing started with Nazir Ahmad and continued up to the first world war in the same accelaration and style. Nazir portrayed the social conditions of middle class Muslim society and wrote for the first time few remarkable novels on their social and religious problems. He depicted the true picture of the contemporary society and selected common people as the characters of his novels. The themes of his novels were generally based on the different social and religious problems of the day, such as, female education, remarriage of widows, relations between husband and wife, monogamy, problems of domestic life, and political role of Muslims under the British rule, etc. Urdu fiction writers were very much influenced by the English education. Western thought and culture stimulated them to review their own society and literature. Nazir Ahmad wrote, "This literature (traditional) teaches us falsehood and flattery. This literature suppresses and wipes out the real beauty of facts........... excites unwholesome passions. . . . . . . Thanks to the study of English I have gradually come to realise the defects of our literature."[8] After Nazir Ahmad, Sarshar, Sharar

8. Ahmad, Nazir, 'Lecture on Mussalmanon Ki Halat-i-Talim' quoted by Tara Chand, History of the Freedom Movement in India, Vol. II, Delhi, Publication Division, 1967, p. 603.

and Ruswa enriched urdu novel as independent innovators and added a new literary glamour to it. They were all learned men and well acquianted with the English novels. Sarshar himself confessed in the foreword of his novel Fasana-i-Azad that he had adopted the techniques of English novel.

Pandit Ratannath Sarshar (1846-1902) started his career as a journalist in the famous newspaper 'Audh Akhbar', in which his novel of an enormous length 'Fasana-i-Azad' (story of Azad) was published and he became famous in the world of urdu fiction. The theme of his novel was the experience of the individuals regarding the social and cultural climate of Lucknow during his time. He wrote few novels but Fasana-i-Azad became most popular with the unforgettable character of 'Khuji'.

Abdul Halim Sharar (1860-1926) also started his career with the journalism but his main achievement was his historical novels. He wrote more than a dozen of such novels, mainly based on the pattern of Scot's 'Talisman' which he had read during his visit to England. Most of his historical novels were written with a socio-religious background. The general deterioriting conditions of Muslims in India and abroad, the challenge of Christianity to Islam through its missionary activities, charitable reformatory activities of Sir Sayyid Ahmad Khan, Publication of Hali's Mussaddas, and other such socio-religious conditions provided a strong hypothesis and encouraged him to write historical novels. He discussed the glorious days of Islam and described its heroes in order to create a sense of social dignity and religious superiority among the Indian Muslims. But Mirza Hadi Ruswal's masterpiece novel 'Umrao-jan-Ada' (story of dancing girl of Lucknow) gave a new direction to urdu novel. He, for the first time, described the subjective experiences gathered in a particular social environment. His attempt was daring and at the same time a deviation from the contemporary style of urdu novels of that period. Some other novelists who contributed to urdu fiction were Md. Ali Talib and Mirza-Abbas Hossain Hosh. But with the publication of 'Audh Panch' under the editorship of Sajjad Hussain a new wave of change was noticed in urdu novels. This paper occupied the same position in the eviolution of urdu novel as Steel's 'Spectactor' in English novel.[9] Sajjad Hussain wrote a few novels and published them in his paper 'Audh Panch' but he came to the forefront with the publication of 'Haji Bughlol.'

With the beginning of the 20th century urdu novels gained a remarkable popularity among the readers. The early twentieth century witnessed the literary values of Romanticism and that influenced the educated middle classes in India. Hence the first pre-occupation of the novel writers was with love, beauty, women, social reform and humanism. Such novels were written by Maulana Rashidul Khairi, Mohammad Sarfaraz Hossain, Mirza Mohammad Sayeed, Mohammad Mehdi Taskeen, Niyaz Fatahpur, and Premchand. Most of the novelists, however, adopted the same mode of expression as the 19th century novelists. For instance, Maulana Rashidul Khairi and Sarfaraz Hossain wrote novels mostly on the same pattern as introduced by Nazir. Both of them took the problems of women but former touched the social and religious problems of women of the middle class Muslim society while the latter was more interested in the life and problems of the prostitutes. In the same way Mirza Mohammad Sayeed and Mohammad Mehdi Taskin adopted to a great extent the techniques of Ruswa and wrote mainly reformative novels in urdu. But among all these novelists Premchand is most prominent for his individuality and he could bring a literary revolution in the world of urdu fiction. He was the first urdu writer who presided over the conference of progressive writers in 1935 at Lucknow and acquainted his readers with a new trend of thought and expression in urdu novel. He was very much influenced by Tolstoy, Gorki and Gandhi. The account of the rural life and particularly that of the peasants, which one finds in his works is really superb. It undoubtedly proves his long acquintance and close intimacy with the rural sector of our country. Gandhian ideology inspired him to look

9. Farooqui, Dr. Ahsan, "Urdu Novel Ki Tanqeedi Tarikh" (The critical history of urdu novel). p. 188. Adara-e-Farogh urdu' Lucknow, 1962.

towards the villagers and as a novelists he could do justice to the ruralities by exposing their aspirations and frustrations to the literate mass of our country. He has also analysed the socio-economic conditions of the rural society and described the rigid caste system, the pitiable condition of the widows and the pathetic treatment towards her, and the custom of child marriage etc. (He himself married a widow in spite of considerable opposition). In the words of Russel "The one really important novelist of the period is Premchand . . . his Gandhian massage is expressed mainly in tales of peasant life. He knew the life of the peasantry intimately and his best work portrays it extremely well."[10]

The next era of urdu novel started with the emergence of the progressive movement which was the direct impact of Karl Marx (1818-1883), and Sigmund Freud (1856-1939). This was the first organised movement of urdu writers who tried to establish a link between literature and society and hence urdu novel experienced a new change both in themes and treatments. Among the progressive writers Krishna Chandar, Aziz Ahmad, Sajjad Zahir, Khaja Ahmad Abbas etc. exposed the important changes and events within the society caused by the contemporary socio-economic factors. Krishna Chandar alone published more than a dozen novels of different lengths viz. 'Jab Kheth Jage', 'Dil Ki Waidan Sogaeen', 'Ghaddar', 'Sarak Wapas Jati Hai', 'Shikast', 'Ek Gadhe Ki Wapsi', etc. All these novels reveal a deep sense of socio-economic awareness of the changing Indian society. For the first time Krishan Chandar introduced the theme of class conflict into urdu novels. He has a mission to describe the capitalist and the ruling classes in all their brutality and beastiality. Marx's influence was widespread in the early 1930s and still continues, to some extent, in urdu novels. Khaja Ahmad Abbas, an eminent journalist and novelist, also wrote his few masterpiece novels under the influence of Marxian thought such as 'Bomaby Raat Ki Bahon Me', 'Char Dil

10. Russel, R. : 'The modern novel in urdu', "The novel in India : Its birth and development", Ed. by T.W. Clark, London, George Allen and Unwin Ltd., 1970. p. 140.

Char Rahen', etc. He has portrayed the socio-economic conditions of Indian society and has given a pathetic picture of poor people who are the victims of the rich and privileged classes. In the same way Razia Sajjad Zaheer traced the gradual emergence of the communist ideology in the urban setting of India after the partition. Through her famous novel, 'Suman' she threw light upon such a society in which the weaker section came forward and get ready to participate in the class struggle.

Freud's influence on urdu writers can also be marked in the novels of Aziz Ahmad, Ismat Chugtai, Rajendar Singh Bedi, Qurratul-Ain-Hader etc. In late 19th and early 20th century urdu novels were confined to moral and religious themes. But Freudian impact liberated urdu writers from moral and religious tunes and as a matter of fact they started discussing sex with frankness and at the some time in a realistic manner. Aziz Ahmad was very much influenced by Freud. His novel 'Shabnam' is based on the Freudian idea of psycho-analysis. Almost all the characters of the novel and particularly those of Arshed Ali and Shabnam have been tackled in Freudian fashion. The psychological tension of Arshed, while he was moving after Shabnam to know about her love affairs, as described by the author is quite consistent to Freudian idea. Aziz Ahmad could observe every minute thing and never felt any hesitation to describe the sexual realities. His other novels viz. 'Hawas', 'Mar Mar Aur Khoon', 'Aag', and 'Gurez' also reflect the Freudian impact, Ismat Chughtai wrote on wide range of subjects e.g. sex, social problem, politics, the fading world of the past and its loveliness and above all, a glittering sense of practical realism. A new kind of fictional technique known as 'Stream of consciousness' developed to describe themes in urdu novels is the out-come of the Freudian impact on literature. Qurratul Ain Haider adopted this technique and produced masterpiece novels viz. 'Aga Ka Darya', 'Mere Bhi Sanam Khane', 'Chai Ke Bagh', etc. in urdu.

Partition of the country also widened the horizon of the urdu writers. The partition was followed by unprecedented changes and also challenges e.g. colossal transfer of population, wide spread riots, kidnaping and abductions, the decline of old ideals and the emergence of new interrogations which had no ready answers. The communal riots with their viciousness attracted the writers most and quite a number of them attempted to find out some solution of the tension which existed between the two communities. Some of them chose to write about the common elements found in Hindu-Muslim Cultures which took shape in undivided India incourse of the centuries.

The spread of literacy and education, the rapid increase in industrialization and urbanization, and the growth of the middle in come group have brought about a considerable change during the post independence period. A trend of liberalism is obviously marked in different spheres of Indian society. The rigid hierarchical structure of our society, is fast breaking up and the process of the liberation of the women has also now acquired a faster tempo. More and more women are being educated and many of them are taking up independent career. They have started playing an increasingly important role in social life. In fact, the entire code of ethical and sexual morality is being challenged. Sex is being discussed with greater freedom and frankness. All these phenomena have brought about a distinct change in attitudes, responses and behaviour which is being reflected in the contemporary urdu novels.

4

Social Situations as Depicted in Novels

In this chapter an attempt has been made to acquaint the readers with the social situations as potrayed in the novels published during the priod under study. The novels, for this purpose, have been selected on a random basis. Moreover, the period of their publication has been taken into consideration. Consequently, some acclaimed novels written by some of the authors could not be included. This limitation of space, at the same time, has made it impossible to include all the noted authors of the period under study.

The analysis of the novels, given below, however, reveals that they have honestly and also in a very realistic manner depicted the social theme of the period in which they were written.

EK CHADAR MAILISI

The novel entitled 'Ek Chadar Mailisi' by Rajendra Singh Bedi is one of the most acclaimed urdu novels of the sixties. On the merit of this novel the author got, in 1966, the Sahitya Akademi Award; the highest literary award in India. The novel was subsequently translated in English by Khushwant Singh.

In this novel the author has introduced his readers to the social life in a Punjab village. The Social scene as depicted seems to be of pre-partition period because the author has shown the Hindus, Sikhs and Muslims are living in the same village as an integrated community. This does not however mean that the social intercourse among the different communities was unrestricted. In fact, it was just otherwise. The Muslims had their own mosque and Mullah in the village and inspite of spatial proximity no inter marriage between the two communities was tolerated. The Muslims were comparatively poor and lived in a hamlet on the out skirts of the village. Here also lived cobblers, washermen and other menials amidst the stench of dung heaps and stagnant sewers. The Muslims, though poor, were very jealous about protecting their dignity being violated by a non-Muslim. They were poor but they never tolerated any outragous attempt against the virtue of any one of their womenfolk. There was, however, no bar regarding the Muslims participating in social ceremonies of the Hindu and Sikh and vice-versa. The young men and women from the different religious communities were friendly to each other. So the situation, as depicted, can be described as a curious admixture of isolation and oneness.

The description of the economic life of the village as given by the author does not give any picture of affluence. The economy was based on agriculture and the economic condition of the common people was not satisfactory. The few rich people, therefore, in many cases exploited the poor. The story of the novel contains the characters of Chaudhry Meharban Das and his brother Chansham Das. Both were rich and indulged in the vices of the wine and women. The common people of the village overlooked their vices but on one occasion both the brothers and a religious mendicant named Babu Hari Das were jailed for raping a minor girl of thirteen. The rich people in the village were in general respected and they had an effective say in village affairs. The traders, shopkeepers, and millers were respected by the common people because of their high economic status. The main economic activity of the villagers was centered round agriculture but the poor and landless often used to supplement their income by manual labour or other activities like driving 'Ekka' etc. In this particular novel the author has pointed out that quite a number of young men of the village Kotla were engaged as Ekka drivers. They possessed their own

Ekkas and used to run their families with the money they earned as Ekka drivers. The poor, quite naturally, had an inferior status and consequently they were less respected. The author at one place while describing the joke thrown by Tiloka, the Ekka driver, to Jehlum, a poor woman, reminds the reader about an old saying i.e. 'a poor man's wife is every one's sister-in-law'. According to the author, Jehlum was used to such remarks and she did not bother to look round.

About the religious beliefs and practices the author has particularly mentioned the condition as prevailed among the followers of Hinduism. They were not free from superstitious beliefs and magic. They also had a ready acceptance of mythological stories which explained the origin and importance of different religious places. Kotla, the village described in the nevel, was a place of pilgrimage. There was a shrine of the Goddess. 'It was said that fleeing from her lusty Bhairon; she had then gone on to find shelter in the wilds of Sialkot and Jammu. If one looked up to the north-west could still see a camel hump formation in the range of hills near Dunel. This was the famous peak named after the Goddess Vaishno Devi'.

The women folk of the village were more superstitious and believed in magical powers as well as practices. They did not hesitate to go a religious mendicant for the spells. Women, quite often, liked to apply these spells in order to keep their husbands' attention focused on them. The author has shown how the heroine of the novel, Rano, went to 'the holy man', Hari Das, who had set himself up beneath the leafless Peepal tree. It was said that he wore a steel bracelet around his loins and never looked at women. This was all the more creditable as he was surrounded by hordes of women at all hours of the day and night. Some came to ask for sons and other for medicine for protection against miscarriage. But most of the women came for charms to keep their husbands in their clutches. In many cases the sadhus were not genuine and men of questionable character. Baba Hari Das as said earlier was ultimately arrested by the police due to his involvement in a rape case.

The religious festivals were observed with grandeur and the entire population of the village as well as of the adjoining villages participated in those festivals. The village temple was the centre of such festivals and all people irrespective of age, sex, economic status used to assemble there. The women used to put on their best dresses and enjoyed the festival by singing and dancing. In Punjab villages purdha was particularly non-existent.

The author has also pointed out the importance of Panchayat in village society. The members of panchayat were influential persons and normally the decision of the panchayat was accepted by the people. In some cases the panchyat members did not mind using physical force to make their decision acceptable. In this novel we find Mangal was beaten severely to honour the decision of the panchayat to marry his elderly sister-in-law. The panchayat also looked after the public institutions and religious organisations of the village viz. temple etc.

The author has also revealed the rich store of folk songs and dances found in the rural culture of Punjab. At many places we get references of the various types of songs and dances. They were related to marriage, birth of a child, religious festivals etc. The nursery rhymes were very colourful and the amorous songs in abundance.

Lastly, the author has drawn our attention to the position of women in rural household and particularly in poor families. The lady of the house had to look after the house hold works viz. cooking, cleaning, looking after domestic animals etc. as well as child rearing. Among the poor payment of bride price was prevailing but it was considered as indignified. 'The girls who went to her husband's home as a proper bride used to be received ceremoniously and anointed with mastard oil; she was subjected to friendly banter and is fussed over by her husband's monther; for her there were songs and games; the changing of utensils; gifts for raising her veil; bridal night of jasmine flowers in a room dimly lit by an oil lamp, full of elemental lust and coyness mixed together'. Normally the well-to-do person used to pay the dowry to the bridegroom and rich presentations to the daughter or the bride.

The relationship between the daughter-in-law and mother-in-law in poor homes particularly was not cordial. In case of Rano, the heroine of the novel, we find old Jindan became the traditional nagging mother-in-law. The real cause of the trouble was their poverty'. The father-in-law was more considerate and treated the daughter-in-law with compassion.

The domestic quarrels were numerous and over various issues viz. wine, want of money, and some times infatuation of the husband to other girls, etc.

Finally, the author introduces his readers with the custom of younger brother marrying the wife of elder brother after the death of the later. This was done with the view to save the family from disruption and at the same time to solve the problem of a helpless widow as well as her offsprings. The unsatisfactory ratio of male and female (the latter being low) also might have the prevalence of such a custom.

AZRA

Saleha Abid Hussain is considered as one among the few urdu novelists who started a new trend in urdu literature. She was deeply influenced by the various socio-economic and political movements of her age. The impact of Gandhian philosophy can easily be traced in her writings. She started writing short stories and novels when India was fighting for independence. Azra is her first novel which was published by Kitabi Dunya Ltd; Delhi, in 1947.

This novel reveals the condition of the Muslims belonging to the middle class at Delhi during pre-independence period i.e., the last phase of British rule over India. The structure of the narration can be divided into three parts viz. 1916 to 1922; 1923 to 1928, and 1929 to 1931. The author has given an account of the conflict between the conservative and progressive Muslim families of Delhi during that period. That was the age of conflict and chaos for the Indian Muslims. The Muslim community was divided into factions on the basis of both religious and social questions. The conservative Muslims were opposed to radical changes caused by the impact of Western education. They refused to accept the English education as it tended to weaken the faith of the Muslims in Islam. On the other hand another group of Muslims, so called progressive Muslims, were the patrons of Western culture and education. The supported female education and became critical of the traditional way of life.

Azra, the heroine of the novel, was born in a conservative Muslim family where women were supposed to bear child, cook food for their husbands and to gossip with their neighbours. They were orthodox in their ideas and attitudes. Azra's father, however, was very much progressive as he got his education in foreign land. He wanted to change the old pattern of thinking in Muslim community but due to his sudden death the mission was left unfulfilled. His wife Nasima decided to take up the mission of her husband and complete it. Though she was also a product of the most conservative society but after marriage she was very much influenced by the dynamic personality of her husband. She did not care for the criticism of others and educated her children up to a higher standard. By that time Sir Syed Ahmad Khan's movement for socio-cultural and particularly educational reforms was started and gained much popularity. He had realised that the lack of Western education among the Indian Muslims was responsible for their backwardness and also for the moral and spiritual decline of Muslim elite. He endeavoured to place reason over faith and superstition. The Muslims society by that time became tradition oriented and the people were motivated more by superstitions than reason. Sir Syed Ahmed with an intention to emancipate their minds from the shackles of the old conceptions laid emphasis on English education and branches of knowledge developed in Western countries as subject matters of study including Islamic theology. After his death his educational reform movement was accelerated by his staunch followers. Nasima was every much influenced by this educational movement and she opened a school in her village where there was no such institutions to impart education to boys and girls. Though she was not fully qualified but she used to teach the students according to her ability. Azra also got her education under the guidance of her mother and passed matriculation examination from

Delhi. She was an extra-ordinary student and she developed an aptitude for writing essays and short stories. But she did not send those articles and short stories for publication as it was thought out of dignity for a girl or a married woman to publish articles and short stories in her own name. The women had no freedom and they used to observe purdah strictly. Naturally their activities were also confined to the walls of their homes. The authoress has acquainted her readers with the prevailing conditions of Muslim women in India before the achievement of Independence through Azra who felt that not only their bodies, but souls, minds as well as thinking were tied with the chains of slavery. But Azra, a girl of middle class Muslim family, accepted the changing pattern of society and refused to be guided by the traditional way of thinking and turned her life towards a new direction. She received education, wrote articles, edited journals as well as newspapers.

The authoress has also depicted the true picture of Independence movement and she has exposed the general feeling of Muslim youths who wanted to sacrifice their lives for the cause of the country. At that time a section of the Muslim community was sympathisers of the British Government. They imitated British culture and took higher education in order to get higher positions in Government. On the other hand another section of the Muslim community took part in freedom movement and sincerely attempted to put an end to the British rule over the country. A number of Muslim youths as examplified in the character of Ansar, Azra's husband, refused to go to England for taking a degree in Law, which was popular among the anglicized Indians and preferred to read such subjects as journalism with an intention to serve the country. In March, 1930, when Mahatma Gandhi started the Civil Disobedience Movement the Independence movement reached at its climax. Freedom fighters became active, processions were organised, public opinion was mobilised and the whole nation became united for achieving independence. The Muslim youths never lagged behind. They took active part in the movement. The educated among them wrote appreciable articles in urdu journals with a view to disseminate the spirit of independence among the members of Muslim community.

Muslim freedom fighters were arrested and sent to jail by the British authorities.

The Muslim ladies could not remain as silent spectators. They broke the taboo of seclusion and stood by the sides of their brothers and husbands and fought for the independence of the country. They boycotted the use of foreign clothes and adopted Khadi. They also took leading role for popularizing Khadi among common people. In a number of cases they did not hesitate to court arrest and went to prison. Those who could not actively participate in the movement became a source of inspiration for their husbands and most of them felt elevated when their husbands went to jail.

The novel, apart from the description of the participation of Muslims in national liberation movement, also acquaints the readers, as said earlier, with the socio-cultural set up of the middle class Muslim families of Delhi during that period. The account given by the authoress is so comprehensive that even the minute items have been missed. In this sense the novel can be described as a social document, very much helpful for learning about the customs and traditions of Muslim community. At one place in the novel we find a detailed account of the marriage practices, particularly dowry, in a middle class Muslim family. The dowry included 20 Joras (Suits)—5 cotton suits and 15 silk suits—bed, quilt, bed covers, pillow covers, table covers, khanposh, handkerchiefs, socks, buniyan, kamarband, 75 pieces of utensils made of Bronze, 25 pieces of crockery and one tea set. The ornaments included 2 Necklaces, 2 earings, buttons, 3 rings and 3 pieces of silver ornaments. The account also give an idea about the guests, the attires of the bridegroom and also the menu of the dinner given on the occasion.

The novel deals with the various changes taking place in the social, cultural and political spheres of the country as well as the reactions of the muslim community towards these changes. The major political movement of that period viz. the movement launched by Indian National Congress and the Khilafat movement have also been discussed in the novel.

After the Sepoy mutiny in 1857 the glory of the Muslim power in India went into oblivion. Gradually the Muslims of

India unconsciously started developing a defeatist mentality and sense of slavery. When the political movements were launched in India against the Britishers a section of the Muslims were awakened and wanted to gain freedom from foreign rule. The conservatives among the Muslims, in spite of the atrocities committed by the Britishers and inhuman torture inflicted upon the revolutionaries, sided with them. Majority of the people, however, imbibed the spirit of revolution and mustered sufficient courage to defy the police force of British administration. They also developed an inclination for Khadi and started putting it on in place of foreign made texture. Spinning was considered to be a moral obligation by these people.

Education of the girls, in middle class Muslim families, was not encouraged. They were denied any type of education except the traditional one or in other words theological. People, however, developed more rational way of thinking and started appreciating the utility of female education and particularly the spread of western education introduced in India by the Britishers. They also could realise the significance of English language which acted as a vehicle for transporting the newly discovered ideas in the western world to Indian mind. Knowledge of English became essential for those who wanted to know about the literature of the different countries of the world. The public opinion, therefore, naturally demanded the spread of English language and literature to the people of this country—both male and female.

MERE BHI SANAM KHANE

Quarratul-Ain-Haider is one of the prominent urdu novelists who worte consistently about those elements of Indian culture which could make the ties between the Hindus and Muslims closer in pre-independence period. These trends could develop in course of centuries and minimised the gulf between the two major religious communities living in this country. The novels written by the authoress reveal a deep sense of secularism, humanism and social justice.

In her novel, Mere Bhi Sanam Khane, the authoress has discussed various dimensions of Hindu-Muslim interaction in our society as well as the partition of the country and its consequences. She has also discussed about the impact of western culture and education on the upper strata of the Muslim community e.g. the landlords, and the changes in the values regulating the status of women in that strata. The rural social atmosphere in pre-partition days has been described and at the same time the sketch of the life in urban centre, particularly Lucknow, given in the book, has made the distinction between the two sectors quite obvious. The in-flow of the refugees and their accommodation as well as the communal riots in India immediately after the partition has not escaped the attention of the authoress. She has mentioned a good deal about the political activities in Uttar Pradesh during the few years preceding the partition.

The authoress very rightly claims that the British rule in India, at least on Cultural level, could minimise the gulf between the Hindus and the Muslims. Though it can not be denied that such trends started developing centuries ago but the process was accelerated due to the diffusion of the liberal thought and secular culture as well as democratic ideals of the west in India.

The western education could infuse a wave of liberalism in Indian society and even the Muslims, who were comparatively more conservative, started changing their outlook on matters relating to female education, seclusion of women etc. In short, it can be said that the spread of western education and particularly in the upper strata of the Muslim community could being radical changes in the status of women in that community. The women from such families were permitted to come out of seclusion, which previously was considered as a mark of nobel genesis, and took part freely in the activities outside their family circles. The removal of a number of restrictions on their movement, the spread of education, acquaintance with the wider world outside their homes and fellowship with the males in the matter of recreation as well as in many forms of social activities helped those women to develop a balanced personality quite different from their preceding generation. Moreover, these educated and at the same time enlightened women developed a sense of secularism and also worked for the removal of the difference between the Hindus and the Muslims.

In her description of the rural life in India during pre-independence period the authoress has pointed out that the villages were divided into small hamlets and in different hamlets people belonging to different castes and religions were living. The Hindus, as now, were divided into different castes and sub-castes both upper and lower, as well as maintained a distance from the Muslims. While describing the life of a village in Uttar Pradesh she has given a fairly long list of different castes living in that village viz. Thakur, Kaistha, Chowdhuri, Hajjam, Jolha, Bhat etc. But inspite of such divisions and sub-divisions there existed in the village a deep sense of emotional integration. The communal sentiment was almost non-existent.

The authoress also has described the various socio-economic changes which took place in the rural sector of our country under the Britishers. In the villages adjoining the cities a lot of changes took place because of electrification, introduction of radio, establishment of educational institutions, availability of modern medical facilities etc.

The picture of the urban life given by the authoress also point out to the absence of hatred among the religious communities towards one another. Speaking about the social life of Lucknow, one of the major cities of Uttar Pradesh, she says that most of the rich people and landlords preferred to reside in the city and there was complete communal harmony. The festival of Muharram was celebrated by both Muslims and Hindus. Hindu women in groups moved on the roads and lanes of the city singing 'Noha' in Purbi dialect. The Muslim landlords in most of the cases used to appoint Hindu Kayasthas as their managers or Munshis, as they were called.

The partition of the country, however, completely reversed the relationship between the two communities. The Muslims were deprived of their social status and were looked down upon in every sphere of life. A large number of Muslims employees were retrenched by their Hindu employers. A new wave of thinking developed among the Hindus which made them consider the Muslims as foreigners in this country having no right to stay here. The entire business run by Muslims collapsed and they developed a sense of fear as well as frustration. As a matter of fact, they removed their name plates from their houses and travelled in trains or buses in disguise of Hindus.

In her description about the political activities during the few years preceding the partition of the country, the authoress has pointed out the agitation launched by the Muslim League for the creation of a separate homeland for the Muslims on the one hand and the activities of Hindu Mahasabha creating a sense of hatred towards the Muslims in the minds of the Hindus on the other. In Uttar Pradesh a large number of Muslims were organized under the leadership of Chaudhri Khaliqquzzaman and on the other hand the Hindus were united under the banner of the Hindu Mahasabha. In short the polarisation of communal forces were taking place in both the communities. With the creation of Pakistan communal riots broke out on a large scale. It was an unfortunate event which swept away all those emotional integrations which existed between the Hindus and the Muslims.

The authoress has depicted the true picture of the communal riots which broke out at Delhi. The streets and lanes of the city were besmeared with blood and covered with dead bodies. The "Supreme Defence council" became ineffective. Jawahar Lal Nehru burst into tears when he could come to know that "Maktab-e-Jamia" was set on fire. He described the Maktab as the precious wealth of the nation.

Many political leaders, prominent among them were Mahatma Gandhi and Zakir Hussain, tried hard to put a stop to the communal riot. Gandhi wept for the loss of human lives. He stood on the stairs of Jama Masjid and tried to console the helpless Muslims girls and women. Zakir Hussain rendered a Yeoman's Service to the riot affected people. He moved all over the riot affected area and distributed food among the people. Some dishonest persons among the Muslims did not hesitate to sell the bread received from Karachi as donation for the affected Muslims in India at exhorbitantly high rate near Purani Qila at Delhi. The riot affected people were also given shelter in tents erected in the compound of the bunglow in which Rafi Ahmed Kidwai was living. A large number of policemen belonging to Muslim community, according to the authoress, also were dismissed from their services.

The partition of the country brought a great change in socio-economic, political, and emotional aspects of life of the people. Influx of refugees added a new dimension to the multitude of problems created by the partition. The population, particularly in urban area, increased suddenly with the arrival of the refugees from Pakistan and these people were harboring a deep sense of hatred for the Muslims. The hordes of refugees consisted of people belonging to different social stratifications. The poor and helpless among them were given shelter in refugee camps organised mostly in the suburban areas of the cities, and the rich were living either with friends and relatives or in hotels. The refugees belonging to the latter category were very much comfortable and used to live luxuriously. They spent money over wine and women and their wives and daughters were attending social gatherings and danced in hotels or clubs. The rich among the refugees also started business and were given big contracts by the Government. They either occupied or purchased propertises owned by the Muslims in minimum price. But the accommodation of the refugees within the local society was not very easy. A sense of difference or a distance emerged in between the local and the migrated people. They were different in many ways. Their language, for instance, was different, and so also the culture. The gulf widened and the local Hindus, after the communal frinzy subsided, felt them more closer to local Muslims than the Hindu refugees from Pakistan.

BATWARA

This novel deals with the changing social values as well as the difficulties faced by the refugees in their adjustment within a new society and culture during the post partition period.

The author C.L. Kavish has rightly observed that most significant change took place in our value structure, is the economic crisis which followed the partition made the people more and more money conscious and materialistic in their outlook. Large number of people were uprooted from their places of habitation and lost their social status. These people were forced to migrate to places not known to them previously and amongst such people who differed in many respect from them. As a result of economic crisis, an anomaly within the society increased and at the same time a number of new opportunities opened up in the society. Even the enlightened section of the people among the refugees started amassing money without any consideration for the means adopted for that. The political turmoil had devastating effects on the humanitarian considerations and the anomaly encouraged them to break all the ethical restrictions which could control their behaviour pattern previously. The most prominent among the vices which developed in the society was 'black-marketing'. It became rampant among the businessmen and their number increased to such an extent that the honest businessmen were driven out of the market. It seemed that the Gresham's law started operating in the business circle and the good coins were ousted by the bad ones. In some cases the honest businessmen were harassed and even murdered by the hired miscreants of the blackmarketeers.

The availability of easy money led to the rise in the standard of living and at the same time made people self centred. This again had an adverse effect on human relationship and the family structure in particular experienced rapid transformation. When the refugees had come to this land they were living under economic strain and also surrounded by numerous problems. All the members of a family had to toil hard and in fact their industrious habit in large number of cases could bring them out of the bad days. But when they could accumulate money by means of black marketing or other unapproved means, they developed individualistic tendencies and the joint family structure started dwindling. The women folk in many cases added incentives to the dividing tendency. The greed for money, lust for a decent, luxurious and comfortable living as well as the control which they exercised over their husbands could enable them to hasten the breakdown of the joint family structure in large number of cases.

The author has, infact, appreciably observed the problems of the refugees who had migrated from Pakistan. The transfer of population, according to the author, produced unprecedented charges in the lives of the people all over and particularly in the younger generation among the refugees who formed a new class of traders and businessmen. This new class of businessmen were fully materialistic and wanted to regain the loss which their elderly people had to sustain as a result of partition. Black marketing, as said earlier, hoarding and bribery etc. appeared as new features within the society and the traditional as well as ethical values were seriously damaged.

Psychologically also the refugees felt themselves isolated after coming to the new land. People not only had lost their lives but those who could escape death had lost their cultural heritage. Loss of culture is definitely very difficult to regain. They found it difficult to adjust with the local people as well as culture and were sentimentally attached to the land which they were forced to leave. The social and emotional maladjustment, therefore, turned the refugees into a miserable lot of people.

PAHLA AUR AKHRI KHAT

The author of this novel, Qazi Abdus Sattar, is one among those urdu novelists who have depicted the situations in rural society in their works. In this novel the author has described the deteriorating conditions of the Muslims landlords in the post-independence period and particularly in Uttar Pradesh.

Partition of the country and abolition of Zamindary system which followed it, has caused a lot of transformations amongst the feudal lords or Zamindars in this country. Quite a large number of Muslim Zamindars have migrated to

Pakistan. Those who are left in India are trying to maintain their old mode of living in spite of the fact that the abolition of Zamindary system has reduced their income to a considerable extent. The author has pointed out that these people have not been able to mould themselves according to the changing situation and most arrogantly trying to hold on their past glory and luxurious way of living even by incurring debts against their properties. They seldom try to augment their income but can not stop being extravagant. They are forced to sell their belongings and also the ornaments or jewelleries of their wives and daughters for money. Wine, women and other aristrocratic pastimes like bird shooting or hunting of wild games are considered as necessary items for maintaining their glory and status. Even now they consider themselves as superior to the common mass of people and avoid social intercourse with them. Marriage of a girl belonging to a Zamindar family with a commoner, though superior in all respects viz. economic, education etc. in many cases is treated as indignified. Consequently, such girls inspite of their attributes viz. physical charm and educational attainments, are left as spinsters. The sons of the zamindars also follow the suit of their fathers and in many cases become addicted to wine and prostitution. The zamindars, in spite of their decaying economic condition, are polygamous. But for procuring a wife they are to enter into wedlock sometimes with girls of the families much inferior in status. The enlightened and well to do middle class parents do not consider these zamindars as suitable matches for their daughters. Such women from the lower class homes at times can not change their former habits even after their entry into the 'Haveli' of the zamindars. We get such an example of Nawab Sitwat Rasul, in the novel, who had married such a girl and she did not hesitate to enjoy sexual intercourse even with the servants of the 'Haveli'.

Thl author has also acquainted the readers with the attitude of the villagers towards these feudal lords or zamindars. It is a fact that the common people in a village are divided on the issues of religion, caste, sub-castes etc but inspite of their differences they respect and seldom try to dishonour these zamindars. Even in the changed context of the situation they sometimes tolerate the high handedness of the zamindars.

From the description given by the author it appears that the sense of defeatism, inability to adjust with the changing situation and above all the fool headedness of the zamindars are the causes leading to their pauperisation.

KALE KOS

This novel by Balwant Singh tells the tragedy which came as a result of the partition of our country. It virtually swept away the Hindu-Muslim amity which took shape in undivided India in course of several centuries. Before partition there was a deep sense of communal harmony and emotional integration but that was badly affected by the different political parties which emerged with communal spirit and programmes. As a result, whole of the sub-continent came under the grip of communal tension. Looting, arson, and killing became quite common. Partition was, however, never demanded by the common people but it was the game of the few narrow minded politicians who wanted to establish their own footings on the national platform by instigating the common people and playing with their sentiments.

The novel introduces the readers at first to the situation which existed in rural Punjab (Now West Pakistan) during pre-partition period. At the second stage there is a description of the accumulation of tension and the activities of the different elements within the society and lastly, there is a narration of the inhuman acts which followed the partition of the country.

Speaking about the rural society in undivided Punjab the author has tried to reveal the communal harmony which existed among the people belonging to different religious communities viz. Hindus, Muslim and Sikhs, living within a particular village. The brotherhood was not essentially confined within the limits of a particular village but infact all the people of the adjoining villages of a particular area considered themselves as members of a single fraternity.

Inspite of the religious differences the social distance was not much and the people belonging to the different religious communities ungrudgingly took part in the religious ceremonies. fairs etc. of one another. Numerically the Muslims were the largest community but that was not the cause of any inconvenience to Hindu or Sikhs. The problems of the village were discussed jointly and men from different religious communities frequently visited the Baithkas (drawing rooms) of each other. In such Baithkas only differentiation which used to be observed was related to Hukka. The Hindus and Muslims were using different Hukkas.

The people were generally orthodox in manners and conservative in outlook. They resisted the new trends or the forces of modernization and treated them with extreme skepticism. They resisted even the opening of educational institutions and hospitals in the village and had no faith in land reforms or economic development in a planned way. They were contented with their respective conditions because they considered that as the desire of God. Female education was not preferred much and they discarded the idea of young unmarried girls living away from their parents and accepting professional career.

Regarding the communal tension which accumulated in the society the author points out that the different political parties were responsible for instigating the communal sentiment of the common people and the city of Lahore, in undivided Punjab, was the most important centre of such activities. The bigots and also the miscreants, who were in search of opportunity tried to inspire the people on communal issues but there were also a large number of such people who resisted the spread of communal feeling. At some places the sincere efforts of such persons could save the lives of the people. But in general the miscreants and also the opportunists could win over the people's mind. As a result the gulf between Hindus and Muslims became apparent and gradually it widened. The country was ultimately divided and communal riots broke out in Punjab. The news of riots in many parts of India viz. West Bengal, Bihar etc. reached there in an exaggerated form and that increased the ferocity of the riots.

The common people fought with each other without realising that the entire plan of communal upsurge was hatched by the British imperialists. People refused to pay any heed to the appeals made by the same elements of the society and ultimately the minority communities from each part left for the other in order to save their lives. But majority of them believed that the situation would some day come to normal and they will be back to their villages. Due to this belief many of them left all their belongings, except ornaments and cash money, at the time of migrating. Those people were sent by special trains but most of them were massacred before the trains could reach their destinations. Their belongings were looted and the women were raped or kidnapped.

PIGHALTA KHAB

The author of the novel, Hamdi Kashmiri, is one of the prominent urdu novelists. In this novel he has described the position of women among the Muslims of Kashmir. He has drawn a comparative picture of the status enjoyed by the women in affluent and non-affluent classes.

The Muslim families in the non-affluent section namely the middle and poor classes are orthodox in their outlook and this provides enough scope for exploitation of the females. They have no freedom of choice in selecting their partners and act according to the commands of the elders. The emotions or preferences of the girls are not given any significance. In case of any disobedience of on the part of the girls the eldors quite frequently use physical force to bring them to senses.

The relationship among the spouses is of dominance and subordination. The husband is the lord and he is unwilling to give equal status to his wife. The wife is considered as a commodity under exclusive possession of her husband. Behaviour of the master to his maid is not always cordial and sometime he does not hesitate even to hit her physically. The wife has no right to criticise the actions of her husband and in no case she is supposed to leave her husbands home without his consent. The parents practically disown their daughter after marriage and in no case they dare to give shelter to their married daughter against the wish of their sons-in-law. Moreover, any misbehaviour on the part of the daughter to her husband brings indignity to her parents. Her primary duty is to please her husband.

Education of the females is not considered necessary and in most of the cases they are not properly educated. This has made them completely dependent on the males for their subsistence. 'Purdha' is another evil which also deserves mention in this connection and polygamy can not be left out of the list of variables causing degradation of females in the society.

The affluent section among the Kashmiri Muslims are much westernised and the position of women in this section is quite different from that one finds in the middle and poor classes. Imitation of western manners and way of life have caused these people to accept the liberation of women. 'Purdha' is almost non-existant among the women in this class and they have full liberty to move in the society. The people belonging to this section mostly live in the city of Srinagar and the impact of urban ethos is clearly marked among them. The young people quite frequently indulge in drinking and frequently visit the hostels, bars or social gatherings. The young ladies also make themselves up accordingly. In some cases they have a number of 'boy-friends', and they go to cinema, hostels and bars with them. The chances of extramarital sexual relationships and prohibited romances can not be ruled out in such situation. Sometimes the fast life and permissive nature of the society lead to sexual imbalance or perverted sexual desire. In many cases such people develop hetero-sexual tendencies.

The author has also drawn the attention of his readers toward the acute unemployment among the younger people belonging to the middle and poor classes of the Muslim families living in Srinagar—the capital city of Kashmir. Majority of them are forced to engage themselves in the fruit-business which is not always sufficiently remunerative. Non-availability of jobs naturally causes deep sense of frustration and despair in the minds of these young people.

RAAT ANDHERI HAI

In this novel, the author Mahinder Nath, has discussed various problems viz. unemployment, slum and other vices prevailing within the society. He has, on the one hand, drawn the picture of the poor and middle class people and on the other he has described rich people and the consequences of too much of affluence. He has also eulogized the Indian womanhood.

The author has rightly pointed out that during the pre-independence period the people developed almost a belief that the achievement of independence will bring an end of the socio-economic miseries of the people. But in fact the volume of such miseries has inflated in the post independence period. The educated young people belonging to the middle or lower economic stratifications in our country have developed a deep sense of frustration and the major variable is the problem of unemployment. In most of the cases such young people do not have soaring expectations rather their ambitions are quite moderate. Most of them want a comfortable living with optimum amenities viz. an attendant for the old parents, good match for his sister and a life partner of his own choice and the like. But in majority of the cases the young man's wishes remain unfulfilled after he finishes his education and fails to find a suitable job.

The independence has not yet been able to improve the lot of the common people. They are deprived of even the bare necessities of life viz. food, clothing, shelter and medicine. The feudal economy of the pre-independence period has been replaced by capitalist economy. This might have happened due to some lacuna in socio-economic transformations during post independence period. Wealth of the nation could not be equitably distributed. The concentration of wealth, and consequently power, has led to the exploitation of the mass in various ways by the capitalists. The urban industrial society which has grown after independence is characterised with unemployment, exploitation, growth of slum, health hazard and many other socio-economic problems.

The industrial urban centres have definitely increased job opportunities but not in proportion to the job seekers. Large number of educated youngmen come to these centres but only a few fortunate among them can find out suitable jobs and the rest have to face the severity of economic wants and forced to accept the jobs meant for manual labourers. With a meager income they can not think of living in any other area of the city than in the slums.

Slum is a type of habitation which is unsystematic, and heavily crowded and lacks the facilities of sanitation, health, and education. Gambling, prostitution, alchoholism and other such vices are the main characteristics of the slum dwellers. In most of the cases these people develop a sense of defeatism and complex of inferiority.

The description of the affluent section and the consequences of too much of economic affluence, given by the author, is limited to the men belonging to the cine industry of Bombay. In this sphere a cruel law of elimination operates. Quite a number of talented boys and girls are attracted by the glamourous lives of the cine stars but very few can get inside it. Without the recommendation of either a top ranking actor or director it is almost impossible to get a chance to act in the film. Most of the girls lose their chastity and instead of becoming a cine star they turn into prostitutes under the pressure of adverse circumstances. In most cases the boys with talent can secure only minor assignments and remain un-noticed throughout their lives.

The dominant ethics which controls the actions of the persons in the cine industry is the accumulation of money. They do not mind adopting any means for their end. The women also have no scrupple in the matter of earning and accumulating money. In other words their concept of life is completely materialistic and quite different from our society. Whoever enters into the arena adopts the same pattern of life in order to survive in that society. The lust for money makes them forget all other virtues of life. They discard their relatives and forget beloveds and in some cases do not hesitate even to commit the most henious crime like murder to remove the barriers to money earning.

Lastly, the author has eulogized the virtues of our women folk. He has rightly pointed out that the women are more sincere in their approaches to their life partners than the men. They can leave their parents and homes as well as make greater sacrifices for their husbands and lovers. Moreover, inspite of betrayal or apathetic treatment by the latter they seldom think of desertion or breaking up the relationship.

SHAMA HAR RANG MEN JALTI HAI

The author of the novel, Thakur Punchi, has narrated the value of art and literature as well as the condition of the artists and writers in the contemporary society. According to him art is no more considered for the sake of art alone rather more emphasis is given on its commercial value. The same is true about the literary works. Moreover, the artists and the writers are to depend on the rich people or capitalists for their subsistence and the latter often exploit their talents for earning handsome amount of profit. In short, the author laments on the condition of artists and writers in contemporary society and points out the evil effect of the commercialisation of art and literature.

People living within a capitalist society are generally materialistic in their approach. In such a society the utility of any thing is judged by the amount of consumer's surplus it provides and in most of the cases the surplus is counted in terms of worldly pleasure on satisfaction. The ethical values in pre-capitalist society were the measuring rods for the efficacy of any object or idea but the capitalist society has a different measurement. The ideal-type of the capitalist society has deviated totally from the religious ethics or ideals and it has become very much intimate to instinctive desires and their satisfaction. Sex and the satisfaction of sex have, therefore, important consideration in the contemporary society. The works of artists and writers are naturally judged from these angles. The author is forced to write sexy stories and the artists can not survive wihout drawing the vulgar portraits of the naked women. Often these works are unrealistic because the artist draws these portraits on the basis of sheer imagination and also for the sake of money.

The author has rightly pointed out that art and literature in the contemporary society are considered as profession and the commercialization of art and literature has created unhealthy effects. The talented persons in these spheres find it extremely difficult to expose their talents. The works of real merit are seldom appreciated and as a result mostly vulgar and debased varieties are produced.

MASOOMA

Ismat Chughtai is considered as one of the most significant women writers of urdu literature. Her novels reveal a wide range of subjects viz. sex, social problems, politices, the receding world of the past and its appreciable features and above all, a sense of practical realism. Her novel 'Masooma' reveals the under current of life in the affluent section as well as the position of the weaker sex, particulrly in the Muslim Community, in the present day Indian society. This novel was published in 1962.

The writer has protrayed a realistic picture of the upper class society of Bombay. Money making is their prime objective and their entire activities are centred round wealth, women and wine. The class consists of big businessmen, financiers of cine Industry, bureaucrats as well as importers and exporters. In spite of professional differences the persons belonging to the class have a common culture, way of life, and outlook. Irrespective of the nature of profession the members of this class considers profiteering above all their goals of life and also develop a hankering for a high status in the society. Lust for money and particularly the greed for profit something make them highly unscrupulous and they do not hesitate to break the ethical norms of the society.

Money in the materialistic society as we have at present, wields an influence and the possessor of money is ensured of a high status. It is, therefore, quite coherent with the situation that the people belonging to the upper class are considered to be the persons of high status. Apparently they are quite magnanimous and often found spending large sums in charitable as well as welfare activities. They patronize orphanages, run widow asylums, give charities and donations and often act as benevolent workers to protect the interest of the weaker section of the people. Many of them, due to their monetary status, become chairman of the organizations and presidents of the public meetings. They know the art of sheding crocodile's tear for the poor and deliver eloquent speeches against social maladies. But behind the screen of maganimity these people move with all ferocity of wild beasts and constantly look about the opportune moment to fall upon the prey which consists mostly of innocent girls of orphanages and helpless women of widow asylums. Underneath the masks of 'Desh Sevaks', 'Social Workers' and 'Nationalists' these rich people commit all sorts of vices. They lure the girls with a prospect of a life full of glamour and comfort and ultimately play with their youth and virginity. Sometimes they spend money to teach the art of coquetry to girls and employ them to exploit the bureaucrats and other men in power in order to obtain contracts, permits, and other privileges. Masooma—the heroine of the novel—is one such girl employed by Raja Sahib for winning the favour of high officials to run his industries smoothly.

These rich people are also in the possession of huge amount of black-money and sometimes aspire to have a place in the political structure of the country. They often contest for seats in the state assemblies or parliament and spend a large amount of black money to purchase the votes or moulding the public opinion in their favour.

The authoress while describing the socio-economic conditions of the people belonging to the right class of people, their psycholgical make up and instinctive activities, have, also revealed the situation of sexual imbalance as well as the exploitation of the weaker sex by the stronger, as prevailing in the Muslim community. This is a vestige of the feudal society. The women are subjected to all sorts of restrictions and follow all the ethical and religious norms. Males on the other hand are more free in their actions and choices. All the religious formalities viz. Namaz, Roza, Haj and others are observed in the Muslim families but the vices of alcohol and sex are also quite rampant. The male is allowed to keep a number of wives and any number of maid servants he likes or affords to maintain. He can not, obviously, satisfy all these women and consequently illicit sexual relationship grows inside the four walls of the house. In the novel we come across the character of Huzur Ali who made a public statement that he had grown old and any child born thereafter in his harem should not be considered as his off spring. The woman reared up in such a situation definitely bears some impact on their personalities and become attracted to the life of vices.

Desertion of women by their husbands is not entirely unknown in Muslim families. These victims of desertion are often dragged to the whirilpool of debauchery and all other forms of sexual perversions. The prevailing practice, so far as sex is concerned, is quite contradictory in Muslim families to the teaching imparted to the females in their early ages. Modesty is a value both in respect of dress and manner. The woman is supposed not to expose any part of their bodies and to consider chastity as the most precious ornament. A woman may lose her life but the chastity should not be lost. In actual practice, however, many irregularities have crept in.

Masooma, heroine of the novel, was the daughter of a deserted woman. She was brought up in a traditional Muslim family and was expected to lead the life of a domesticated woman. But poverty compelled her to be otherwise. In the highly urbanized and materialistic society she gradually sank deeper into the vicious circle of sex and immorality. Masooma was transformed to Nilofer, the concubine of a rich man and a tool for satisfying the lust of many men. She became an alcohol adict and started drinking so much that in the state of intoxication. 'She could have slept even with a dog'.

The authoress has given a sex oriented detail of the life led by the male in rich strata of the society. She has made no reservation in exposing the lewdness of these people. Her descriptions of sexual orgies and lascivious behaviours of the male are quite lively. Often these behaviours, as depicted in the novel, crosses the limits of normal sexual expression and can be considered as perversions. Exposition of her charms before the males by a female, to demonstrate her youth, and the pride as well as satisfaction associated with it reminds the reader of Freudian impact on the novel. At many places in the novel the authoress has clearly exposed the impact of the Freudian psycho-analytical approach in the writing.

Earlier fictions in urdu literature were very much conservative about the physical aspect of sex and it was covered under a spiritual cloak. The love of a man for woman and vice-versa was purely described as something devoid of physical attraction and more romantic as well as platonic in nature. The impact of Freudian psychology made the novelists more realistic in their approaches towards sex and particularly its physical aspect. Ismat Chughtai is one such convert, and also the first among women novelists in urdu, who does not hesitate to go beyond the traditional limits to discuss the facts of sexual life. This, of course, makes her novels more realistic and adds vitality to her narrations.

BOMBAY RAAT KI BAHON ME

Khaja Ahmad Abbas was an eminent novelist and journalist of India. He wrote a number of fictions both in Urdu and English. He was deeply influenced by Marxian Philosophy and he was one of the important members of the group of progressive writers in urdu literature.

'Bombay Raat Ki Bahon Me' is one of the most popular urdu novels in which the author has portrayed the socio-economic conditions of India's one of the biggest cities, namely Bombay. He has given a pathetic picture of slum life which is the outcome of the present day industrial and urban growth. Bombay is an ocean of human population. Being a centre of employment and business it attracts a large number of people. As a matter of fact these immigrants create a lot of social and economic problems of which two are very important viz. the demand for living accommodation and growth of slums. A large number of immigrants live in 'Lean tos' against walls of mills, factories and residential houses. The author of this novel has described these slums and pavement dwellers of Bombay. These people have no right of occupancy over the land. They are frequently subjected to humiliation and torture by the owners of the land. Their huts are removed or burnt down and reconstructed again and again. They have no protection against these regular threats by the cruel and unsympathetic landlord who treat these helpless and miserable people as very much unwanted. The intention behind these raids by the hired ruffians of the landlords is to evict these slum dwellers and to errect huge buildings which fetch them handsome rents. But they never think of providing any alternative place of living to these poor people.

The author has portrayed the character of such a land lord Sona Das Daleria who is a symbol of modern bourgeoisie found in every metropolitan city of India. Through this character the author has attempted to reveal the realistic picture of the social norms and economic affluence of the class of bourgieoisie living in the city of Bombay. The central theme of this novel is based on the conflict between a journalist and a capitalist. The journalist—Amar Kumar—is honest and quiet efficient in his profession. His articles and comments were read and appreciated by the poorer section of the literate mass. He used to ventilate the pitiable conditions of these people through his writings, living in the slums owned by the unscrupulous landlord Shri Sona Das Daleria. The journalist, however, was a poorman with insufficient income and could not meet even the bare necessities of life. Sona Das Daleria, a shrewd capitalist, wanted to exploit his poverty and offered him the job of Public Relation Officer in his firm with a flat salary of Rupees two thousand and five hundred per month and a well furnished bungalow as well as a car. He tried to purchase the journalist Amar Kumar with an intention to prevent him from writing against him. Amar Kumar represents the poor section of the Indian journalists who has to face not only economic hardships but also the barriers created by the capitalist class of the society. In spite of the freedom of speech and expression guaranteed by the Indian constitution, these journalists have to face a lot of problems created by the capitalist and expoliters of the mass. The author himself is an eminent journalist of India hence his account of these exploitations suffered by the journalists is very realistic.

Bombay is a city of huge population. In this ocean of human beings the numerous socio-economic problems appear like a hydra headed monster emitting venom in all directions. The author, like a Superb artist, has tried to reflect in his literary canvas the entire picture of the social life of Bombay including the numerous problems viz. housing, sanitation, exploitation of the poor and weak section of people by the capitalists, problems of crime and social maladjustment etc.

The strongest ethics, as the author has pointed out in the capitalist class is to accumulate wealth. This ensures the status of a man within his class and all other personal qualities are subordinated to the accumulation of wealth. The disqualifications and personal vices are also ignored in case of a rich man. In this novel we are acquainted with the character of a rich man named Tutu who used to indulge in wine and women. He has such a debauch that he used to invite only those persons in his parties, who could come with their girl friends. Like all other capitalists, Tutu also believed that anything and every thing in this world could be purchased by money. He did not hesitate to cast his lustful eyes on Asha, wife of Amar Kumar, the journalist. He attempted to persuade her to marry him and promised to take her, after the marriage, for a honeymoon to London, Paris or Geneva which the poor journulist could never afford.

The author has also dealt with the problem of crime in the city of Bombay. As a keen observer with sociological understanding the author rightly feels that the criminals are not born but they are made such by the adverse social forces. The criminals are mostly pampered by bourgeois or the capitalists. These unfortunate people in lieu of few pieces of silver commit unlawful activities and the fruits of such endeavours ultimately enrich the capitalists. The criminals in most of the cases procure and supply such articles to the capitalists which are essential for the satisfaction of their instinctive desires. This includes mostly wine and women.

EK LADKI AUR HAZAR DIWANE

This is one of the popular novels of Krishna Chandar, whose name figures quite prominently among the urdu novelists. The book was published in the year 1960. In this novel the author has drawn a picture of the social life among the Gypsies. These people are wanderers and maintain a migratory way of life. They have their own language and religion. Regarding their origin a section of scholars claim that Gypsies are not a pure race rather an admixture of many racial elements. Because of their migratory character they do not have any permanant abode and live in their tents.

The most interesting and striking feature which the author Krishan Chandar has pointed out is about the position of women among the Gypsies. The women have much freedom of movement and action but at the same time they are treated as precious commodities possessed by their husbands. Normally they are monogamous but divorce, separation and in many cases transfer of women from one husband to the other is allowed. The level of morality or chastity of the female from our standard of measurement is quite horrible. The husband does not mind wife going for prostitution to earn money. The wife looks after the household and makes her sincere efforts to provide comforts to her husband.

The Gypsies are poor and their economic activities differ widely from the settled people. The women earn more than the males and because of their economic potentialities they are adored by the males. The males are often idlers and indulge in drinking and gambling. They engage themselves in basket making and weaving mat to earn a little amount. The habit of gambling is so frequent in their community that sometimes they lose everything in their possession, even wives, to the opponent. The heroine of the novel Lachi is seen living with her uncle Maman because her mother was also living with them. Her father Raggi lost his wife (Lachi's mother) and, naturally the infant daughter, to his brother Maman in gambling. Later on Maman also sold Lachi to Dumaru when he had lost much of his belongings in gambling with Dumaru.

They believe that women, mare and land all the three are marketable commodities. They can be sold and purchased.

Other than gambling the favourite pastimes of the males in Gypsy community are dancing, singing and playing on musical instruments like Duff etc. They, however, like best to idle away their time. The lust for money sometimes drag them to criminal ways of earning money like theft, cheating and sometimes bigger offences like homicide etc.

The main source of income in their community are the females. As said earlier, they earn money by prostitution and even indulge in petty thefts. Quite often their women put on colourful dresses made of art-silk and move in lanes and bazars of the city selling mirrors, rings and ornaments made of gilt, herbal medicines etc., and earn a lot of money. They try to attract their customers by exposing their physical charm and amorous postures. Begging is another source of income for the Gypsy women. They are quite apt in the art of begging and the young girls prefer to beg in crowded places of the city like market places, bus stops, railway stations etc.

The author has also mentioned some of the interesting social customs of Gypsy community related to marriage. While arranging the marriage the consent of the bride is not always considered essential. Marriage is a contract and involves monetary exchange. The bridegroom is to pay the bride price and the highest bidder is offered the hands of the bride. The most interesting custom which the author has mentioned is that the bridegroom is to carry the bride from the place of marriage to his own tent by lifting her on his arms. If the bride is unwilling she puts resistance and in case the bridegroom fails to carry her away to his tent he cannot claim her as his wife. Lachi, heroine of the novel, was strong enough to prevent Damuru from carrying her out to his tent and thus saved herself from his clutches. The procedure of marriage in their community is otherwise quite simple and no complicated formalities are observed.

Marriage of a Gypsy girl outside her own community is not prohibited but not much apppreciated. The community is knitted quite closely and the members seldom like to go out of it.

The Gypsies, and especially their women, are very particular about keeping their promises made to any other member of their community. They consider it as sin and humiliating to break promises. In some cases they will give up the happiness of their lives instead of breaking promises.

The story of the novel is like a biography of a Gypsy girl, named Lachi. She is beautiful and young and as such all men she meets look at her with lust and passion. She develops a strong desire for settled life with a home, husband and children. Her sense of sexual morality is quite different from other girls of her community. She fails in love with a non-Gypsy boy named Gul who wanted to marry her. Her love for Gul makes her to kill Dumaru with whom her parents forced her to marry by accepting money. The poor girl is sentenced and while in prison she looses her beauty as well as eye sight due to the desease of small pox. The author thereafter has painted the gloomy and miserable life of Lachi. Every one even Gul deserts her and she drags on her existence as a poor blind beggar.

HAZAAR RATEN

The author of this novel Sheen Muzaffarpuri has described the nature of immoral traffic in women as found in metropolitan cities and particularly in Calcutta. This is a very flourishing trade and sometimes the influential as well as sophisticated persons are the patrons of this trade. The girls are forced to enter into this profession due to various adverse circumstances of life and the most important among them is poverty. The procurers and touts get hold of such girls those who are helpless, unprotected, ignorant or the victims of unscrupulous males, whom they might have trusted, and recruit them as prostitutes.

Our society, due to its male dominated structure, is often quite callous abous giving adequate protection to helpless women. Extra marital sex activities is more strictly forbidden in case of girls then the boys and a poor girl even if she loses her virtue under unavoidable circumstances viz. physical force or deceit, society does not pardon her.

The story of the novel is about a girl named Munni. She is an orphan and also a beggar. The author through this character has tried to explain the sad plights of a poor girl. In spite of all her sincere efforts she could not protect herself from the amorous persons and at the same time could not get a respectable means of subsistence. She even worked as a maid servant but the master's son exploited her and when it came to the notice of the master's wife she was removed from her job. Ultimately the poor girl became a prostitute.

The author has rightly observed that there are numerous Munnis who enter into prostitution under duress and the society instead of giving any protection looks down upon them.

The author has also given an account of the various forms of prostitution found in the city of Calcutta. In some cases even the married women indulge in this profession for the maintenance of their families. Such women are mostly attached to bars, hotels and clubs as 'Call-girls'. At many places the empty rooms are available for the purpose of prostitution in lieu of money. The author has also mentioned about the 'massage and bath' clinics providing prostitutes to their clients. In most of these clinics the prostitutes are employed for massaging and, if the client pays the requisite money, for sexual intercourse.

The author has also made some passing reference about the girls working in the cine industry and also about the beggars of Calcutta.

The beautiful young girls are naturally lured by the grandeur of the cine industry but this is a circle where no girl probably can avoid sexual exploitation. The people attached to this industry are mostly addicted to wine and women. In order to secure contracts in film most actresses have to sleep with the Director or Producers and sometimes with top actors. The glamour of the screen attracts many educated girls of respectable families but once they get into it their dreams are shattered and they virtually lead an ignominious life.

Beggary, according to the author, is a well organised profession. In Calcutta, there are gangs of people who organise and control the profession of beggary. The chief of a beggar gang is in majority of the cases, a strong man with cruel temperament. He gives training to the boys and girls for begging as well as for pick pocketting and cheating innocent people. The beggars also adhere strictly to the rules framed by their chief.

SONA GACHI

Jamana Das Akhtar was an eminent journalist and novelist. He wrote a number of novels covering different aspects of socicty. 'Sona Gachi' is one of his famous novels in which he portrays the lives of the prostitutes. In India like other countries of the world, existence of prostitution could be traced back to the hoary past and still it functions as an important institution particularly in urban and industrial sectors of our country. Sona Gachi, according to novelist, is one of the centres of prostitution in Calcutta. It is a market quite well known for trade in 'Women's Flesh'. The author further says that Calcutta is one of the biggest centre of prostitution in Asia where the business is carried only on a large scale. He also accepts in the preface that the characters and location of the novel are real.

The novelist has depicted the live picture of the prostitutes and their living conditions in the red light area.

The business in a particular area is controlled by a band of old women, extremely shrewd and merciless, but at the same time quite conversant with the many dark alleys through which the professional has to travel. These old veterans generally found as keepers of brothels. They train the girls who are either induced or compelled to join the profession and also give them protection. In lieu of her service she is entitled to a share, sometimes the Lion's share, in the income of these poor girls. In short, the old women act as the matron of the brothel house, in her own manner.

About the clientele of the prostitutes the author has pointed out that it often includes persons with dignity and high level of sophistication. It does not, however, mean that people from ordinary walks of life do not visit the prostitutes. In fact the latter constitute the larger section of those who patronise them.

The police also play their role within the framework of the profession. They are the exploiters and almost essentially claim a share in the income of the prostitutes. The lust for money encourage the police man to prevent the escape of a poor victim of prostitution from the brothel. The keepers of the brothel and sometimes even the clients act in liason with the police man on the street. The police men also demand sexual gratification, just for nothing, and the prostitutes are compelled to satisfy them. The author cites the example of a prostitute named Zarina who while attempting to escape from the brothel was prevented by a police Havildar named Asutosh Mukerjee. The Havildar threatened to shoot Zarina.

The author has also attempted to explain the causes of the emergence of prostitution as an institution in Indian society. He feels that out of the innumerable causes of prostitution the sociological, economic, and psychological factors are more significant.

The growth of industrialization is followed by the establishment of big urban centres with all sorts of complex social relationships and professional organisations. Due to the pull of the city, as a result of growing opportunities of jobs and other life chances, people from far and near emigrate to the city. Quite a large section of these emigrants come to the city alone leaving the female members of their families in villages. These people often visit the prostitutes for sexual gratification as well as release of mental strain caused by the conditions prevailing in cities. Demand for the girls of easy virtue thus increases and consequently in every big city a red light area develops where the girls of easy virtue or in other words the prostitute cater the sexual pleasure to the patrons.

Poverty, according to the author, is the most important contributory factor to the development of prostitution. In many case the pang of hunger forces the girls of poor families to enter into the life of prostitution.

Lure for a glamorous life can also be counted as a cause of prostitution. Young girls are often tempted to enter into the cine industry in order to become heroines in the screen and to lead lives full of glamour. In some cases the temptation is so strong that they run away from their homes only to fall prey in the hands of unscrupulous people and Dalals (brokers). Consequently, they lose their virtues and ultimately find places in city brothels. The fear of disgrace and sense of humiliation deter them from returning to their homes.

A large number of girls, according to the author, are either deceived or abducted and brought to the 'red light' areas of the cities for the purpose of prostitution. These unfortunate girls become absolutely helpless and can not escape from the life of shame and exploitation. Moreover, our society which is dominated by orthodox norms and places too much of significance on sexual purity and chastity do not provide any place to accommodate these poor victims of circumstances.

In this novel we come across the story of a girl named Shanta—daughter of a Professor—who was deceived by one Suresh whom she believed and left her parental home with him to join the film industry. The poor girl was betrayed by Suresh and lost her virtue. She was exploited and at the end compelled to accept the life of a prostitute with a new name—Badarunnisha.

Prostitution, as suggested earlier, is an elaborate organisation and the network is so vicious that even the social workers with sincere zeal find it extremely difficult to break the vicious circle. In the novel we find the effort made by Nagindar Babu, an eminent social worker of Calcutta. He made an attempt to rescue the girls from brothels for their rehabilitation and had to face a lot of troubles. He was assaulted by the brokers and several murderous attempts were made upon his life. But the dauntless spirit of the social reformer could not be tamed by the ruffians. He ultimately succeeded in rescuing few prostitutes from the red light area.

The nevel, considering the above analysis, can be treated as a realistic document of the institution of prostitution and the life of prostitutes in Calcutta, the biggest metropolitan center of our country.

5

Impact of Marxian Idea on Urdu Novels

In the year 1875 the manifesto of the communist party was published in London for the first time. During the preceding year Marx and Ingels were commissioned by the communist league to draw a theoretical as well as practical programme of the party. Marx suggested in this manifesto that, "in every historical epoch, the prevailing mode of economic production and exchange, and the social organisation necessarily following from it, form the basis upon which alone can be explained the political and intellectual history of the epoch consequently the whole of history of mankind (since the dissolution of the primitive tribal society, holding land in common ownership) has been a history of class struggle, contests between exploiting and the exploited, ruling and the oppressed class; that the history of these class struggles forms a series of evolutions in which, now a days, a stage has been reached where the exploited and the oppressed class—the proletariat—can not attain the emancipation from the Sway of the exploiting and ruling class—the bourgeoisie—at the same time, and once and for all emancipating society at large from all the exploitation, oppression, class distinction and class struggle."[1]

Marx propounded a new theory of dialectical materialism. In fact he could get the idea of dialectic in the Hegelian concept of inherent change and applied the same on the

1. Marx, Engels, Lenin—The Essential Left, Unwin Books, London, p. 12, 1950.

social and physical environment. Hegel confined his use of dialectic only within the world of ideas. The Hegelian concept of dialectic actually signifies a process of change in which an entity passes over into and is preserved and fulfilled by its opposites. It is a development through the stages of thesis, antithesis and synthesis. Marx in his theory of dialectical materialism maintained that the material basis of a reality changes constantly in a dialectical process. He also gave priority to matter over mind.

The term Marxism has come to mean many different things. "In his funeral address for Marx, Lenin defined the subject of Marxism as being the law of evolution of human history. If one adds a rider that human societies are characterised by distinct socio-economic structures on which their other aspects depend and that there are specific laws governing the dynamics of every distinct social formation, we have a definition sufficient to distinguish Marxism from alternative approaches."[2] George Lichtheim says, "Marxism can be regarded as one intellectual construction among others; alternatively, it can be assigned a definite place among the socialist movement of the nineteenth century which arose from the impact of industrial revolution on European society."[3] According to Roger Graudy, "Marxism is not one of a number of philosophies but an awareness of the underlying movement that govrens our history."[4]

Marx was materialist in his approach and believed that human actions are generally motivated or conditioned by such material needs as food, clothing, and housing etc. Moreover, he claimed that every society has an economic base. The societies differ from one another on the basis of their respective economic organisation viz. pastoral or hunting and food gathering or built around cottage industries or

2. Schlesinger, Rudolf : Marx—His Time and Ours, Routledge and Kegan Paul, London. pp. 1-2, 1951.
3. Lichtheim, George : Marxism—A Historical and Critical Study, Routledge and Kegan Paul, London, 1961, p. xiii.
4. Graudy, Rogers : Marxism in the Twentieth Century (Translated by Rene Hague) Collin, London, 1970, p. 9.

complex industrial units. "But whatever the form in which men organise to solve their basic economic problem, the society will require a whole super structure of non-economic activity and thought—it will need to be bound together by laws, supervised by a government, inspired by religion and philosophy."[5] Marx considered the ideas as the products of environment, creative and at the same time capable of bringing change in the social order but they are the passive accompaniments of economic activity. According to Marx, "Men make their own history, but they do not make it just as they please, they do not make it under circumstances chosen by themselves, but under circumstances directly found, given and transmitted from the past."[6]

The fruitfulness and creative effectiveness of Marxism have been proved in a number of practical fields. It has liberated millions of men, enslaved for centuries, and given them access to their culture. These liberated people have also won living conditions for themselves that are at least human. Marxism, moreover, has changed the social and economic life of vast countries. "Marx and Engels made man sharply aware of his potentialities and gave the working class a programme for building up a society that would allow man to attain the fullness of his development; and within it, they gave a technique which is both a fighting technique and a sicentific technique for establishing this society...This teaching had begun to organise the class war of the proletariat throughout the world, and to inspire complete confidence in the victory of the labour movement."[7] The term social class indicates, "the aggregate of persons having essentially the same social status in a given society."[8] Marx, however, had given an economic interpretation of social classes. He claimed that class is always a manifestation of economic differentiation. The economic factor is commonly associated with status

5. Heilbroner, R.L. : The Wordly Philosophers, Simon and Schuster, New York, 1953, pp. 135-36.
6. Ibid.
7. Graudy, Rogers : Op. cit, pp. 9-10.
8. Ogburn, W.F. and Nimkoff, M F. : A Hand Book of Sociology, Routledge and Kegan Paul, London, 1950, p. 210.

distinctions, to be sure, and no more markedly than in modern capitalistic society. "Marxian theory, materialistic and economically oriented, views class attitudes and class consciousness as fundamentally a reflection of economic conditions and teaches that the sentiment of corporate unity inevitably emerges within each of the basic economic classes. Yet......the growth of corporate class consciousness does not take place automatically or according to any definite time schedule —thus organizational efforts to solidify the working class.'[9] Marx had rejected all the existing ideas regarding class differentiation in a society and formulated a dichotomus division of social classes viz. Bourgeois and Proletariat. He further said, "Thehistory of all hitherto existing society is the history of class struggles. Freeman and slave, patrician and plebeian, lord and serfm guildmaster and journey man, in a word, oppressor and the oppressed, stood in constant opposition to one another, carried on an uninterrupted, now hidden, now open fight, a fight that each time ended, either, in a revolutionary reconstitution of society at large, or in the common run of the contending classes."[10] By bourgeois is meant the class of modern capitalist, owner of the means of social production and employer of wage labour. By proletariat, the class of modern wage labourers who having no means of production of their own, are reduced to selling their labour power in order to live."[11] Any change in the economic structure, according to Marx, is always followed by a reciprocal change in the class structure within the society. "The present day capitalist mode of production pre-supposes the existence of the two social classes—on the one hand that of the capitalists, who are in possession of the means of production and subsistence, and on the other hand, the proletarians, who are being excluded from this possession, have only a single commodity for sale, their labour power,

9. MacIver, R.M. & Page, C.H. : Society, Macmillan, London, 1955, pp. 361-62.
10. Bierstedt, R. (Ed.) : The Making of Society, The Modern Library, New York, 1959, p. 212.
11. Marx, Engels, Lenin : Op. cit. p. 14,

and who therefore have to sell this labour power of theirs in order to obtain possession of means of subsistence."[12] In the modern capitalist society the class struggle has assumed a simpler form. The classes are differentiated on the basis of their specific economic interest. "The complicated arrangements of the social classes as found in the earlier decades of the history is now being replaced by the sharp distinction between the two social classes of the capitalistic society viz. Bourgeois and Proletariat. Exploitation of the weaker by the stronger is a constant factor in history. The capitalism has created the two great hostile camps—Bourgeois and Proletariat —and new forms of struggle as well as oppression."[13] The existence of the bourgeois class as well as their Sway over the society rest essentially upon the formation and augmentation of capital. "The condition for capital is wage labour. Wage labour rests exclusively on competition between the labourers. The advance of industry, whose involuntary promoter is the bourgeoisie replaces the isolation of the labourers, due to competition, due to association. The development of modern industry, therefore, cuts from under its feet the very foundation on which the bourgeoisie produces and appropriates products. What the bourgeoisie therefore produces, above all are its own grave diggers Its fall and the victory of the proletariat are equally inevitable."[14] The bourgeois and proletariat developed simultaneously in the society.

The proletarians are the working class of our modern society who depends for their survival on the availability of jobs. The capitalists as employers hold the bargaining power by dint of which they can exploit the workers or the proletarians. Gradual increase in the numerical strength of the proletarians create a sense of invincibility in their minds and with a view to avoid exploitation they organise trade unions. These unions endeavour to keep the wage rate high

12. Marx, K. and Engels, F. : Selected Works, Vol. II, Foreign Language Publishing House, Moscow, 1955, p. 49.
13. Mukherjee, R.N. : A History of Social Thought, Saraswati Prakashan, Mussorie, 1960, pp. 115-116.
14. Marx, Engels, Lenin : Op. cit. pp. 26-27.

and for that purpose struggle with the capitalists or the employers. At times the conflict results into sporadic riots. Marx was very much optimist about the ultimate victory of the proletarians over the capitalists because he believed that due to the similarity of interests the proletariat class all over the world will unite and overthrow the domination of the capitalists. The victory of the proletariat will lead to the establishment of the dictatorship of the proletariat over the world. Once the proletariat of the world unite they will forget the regional bias and the nation states will wither away. This idea of Marx revolutionised the entire existing understanding about world history. "The whole previous view of history was based on the conception that the ultimate causes of all historical changes are to be looked for in the changing ideas of human beings and that of historical changes dominate the whole of history. But the question was not asked when the idea came into man's minds and what are the driving causes of the political changes are."[15]

Marx rules out the possibility of a middle class in the society. He identified the middle class with the class of petty bourgeois which developed in those countries where the modern civilization could attain the fullest growth. People belonging to this class in fact fluctuate between the bourgeois and the proletariat and exists as a supplementary part of the bourgeois society. Marx visualised that with the further culmination of capitalistic economy this class of people will be reduced to proletariat and will completely disappear as an independent section of modern society.

Marx also gave a new conception of the term 'Value' which normally conveys the idea of utility and exchangeability of commodity. According to Marx, however, the amount of labour required, whatever may be the form, direct or indirect, for the production of a commodity actually determines the value of the commodity. In other words the commodities are

15. Reminiscences of Karl Marx, p. 25 (An essay by Engels entitled Karl Marx, written in June 1877, Published in the Volk. Kalendar, and almanac which appeared in Burnswicj in 1877) Foreign Language Publishing House, Moscow.

priced by labour alone. The capitalist purchases the labour of the labourer and the competition as well as the barganing power of the capitalist enables him to pay the labourer less than the worth of his labour. The unpaid labour forms the profit of the industrialist or capitalist. Marx explained it as 'surplus value'. He rejected the concepts of the earlier economists like Ricardo and Adam Smith that every increase in the wage of the labourer will increase the out put. Marx said that the capitalists compete with each other for profit and with this motive they expand their scale of production but the expansion needs more labourers. This leads to the increase in the demand for labourers and at the same time their wages also increase. But the increase in wages causes a decline in the amount of profit of surplus value of the capitalist. In order to come out of this dilemma the industrialist or capitalist takes the resources of automation as a labour saving device. The automation of industries leads to unemployment among labourers, formation of the 'industrial reserve army' by the unemployed labourers and also checks the increase of wages above the subsistance level which according to Ricardo is the true value of the labourers.

The machines, according to Marx, are not good substitutes of human labourers so far as the surplus value is concerned. The capitalist or industrialist has to pay almost the same price for the machine which is equivalent to the price of the goods it is capable of producing during its life time. Automation of industries or machanization of the means of production, therefore, 'reduces the number of hens laying golden eggs for the capitalist'. The competition among the capitalist, at the same time, leaves no alternative other than automation for a capitalist and their margin of profit is reduced. The shrinking of profit compels all the capitalists to adopt more cost saving and labour reducing devices. As a result the profit margin shrinks further and a stage comes when practically no profit is left. In order to boost up the sale the bigger industrialists start dumping operation and the small firms are completely ruined. The labourers are compelled to work on lower wages due to slump and the machines also become available on reduced prices. The surplus value or profit reappears for sometimes but the vicious cycle does not stop operating. It is repeated again viz. competition for labourers, higher wages, labour saving machinery, reduction in surplus value, more fierce competition and collapse. East collapse is followed by absorption of more smaller firms by bigger firms. This is the last act of the drama. The size of the working class increases due to proletariatization of the smaller capitalists and along with it the diminishing number of capitalists brings monopolisation accompanied by an augmentation of misery, exploitation, degradation, oppression and slavery. The conflict between the bourgeois and the proletariat at this stage reaches at its climax. Finally, the conflict ends with the victory of the proletariat and the establishment of the 'dictatorship of the proletariat.'

Marx had also given a materialist conception of history. The social relationships, according to this conception, are linked with the forces of economic production and primarily economic in nature. When the forces of production change it brings a rift between the economic factor and economic relationships. The entire social super structure which is based on economic relationship consequeutly changes along with a transformation in the process of production. "But the social or economic order does not conform to the gradual emergence of the economic demand. For the older order has created its ideologies and its vested interests. It is those who are fettered by the now obsolescent order who awaken to the consciousness of its decay and accomplish to its overthrow. A social revolution thus attends the birth of each new stage of society. The ideology of the class whom that order suppressed and when the new would liberate. Thus in the words of communist manifesto, 'the history of all hither to existing society is the history of class struggle."[16]

The real foundation of any society is the economic structure. The legal or political institutions are the specific expressions of social consciousness. The economic structure is determined by the mode of production which again depends on the stage of technical development. Any new development, in

16. MacIver and Page : Op. cit. p. 560.

technology, therefore, induces a similar change in social relationships and institutions. The economic order of a particular society is expressed in its intellectual, spiritual, cultural and aesthetic activities as well as in its philosophy and creeds. Thus, according to the Marxian concept, all thoughts, philosphies, beliefs, art, literature etc. are basically determined by economic facts. They also express the position of the individuals in their class structure. Marx interpreted ideologies as reflection of class interest which differs from the Freudian concept of retionalization.

Marxian philosophy or ideology and particularly the scientific analysis of class struggle produced almost a revolutionary change in the realm of thought. The literary measures were also revolutionized and the modern progressive literature originated at this point. This, however, does not mean that before Marx there was an absence of progressive ideas in our society. In fact they were present at all the stages of our social evolution but the novelty of Marx is judged by his social and political interpretations of the situation. Marx based his concepts on historical and material dialectic and his concepts were accepted by the urdu novelists. In the following tables the content analysis of some major urdu novels bearing Marxist influence has been given.

CONTENT ANALYSIS OF SOME NOVELS BEARING MARXIAN INFLUENCE

Name of the author and Novel

1. *Shakeelur Rahman, 'Naye Farhad'*

The Theme of the Novel

The author is obviously influenced by the Marxian ideology and the story the novel reveals the same. The author has attempted to analyse the extremely unsatisfactory conditions prevailing in our society as well the various socio-economic factors resulting into the exploitation of the larger section of people by a much smaller section of rich and privileged class of people. Economic hardship and poverty as well, act as barriers to the development of robust personality among the lower strata of the society which constitute the larger section of the people in our society.

Deprivation of basic needs and constant struggle for existence against the exploiters create deep sense of frustration in their minds. The instinctive desires and the finer sentiments often get crushed under the pressure of economic wants.

The author with an intention of making the position of the poor section of the people more clear as well as his description more realistic has given an account of the life led by the rich and privileged class in the society. The former section can be identified as the proletariate who depend on the wages they earn by selling their physical labour. The present state of unemployment in our society exposed its capitalistic nature and at the same time the unemployment has provided the rich class or the employer with a power to bargain. This bargaining power of the capitalist is the real source of exploitation of the labourers. The rich or the privileged class can be identified with the bourgeoisie. This class of people play the role of exploitation. The main incentive of this class to earn as much profit as possible and to accumulate money. They do not care for any other ethics and whenever they face an opposition from the labourers, try to crush it with all the might available to them. They often try to win over the opposition by money and when other means fail they do not hesitate to kill the opponent with the help of their hired agents.

The author has also described the role of middlemen in capitalist society. They are the main props of the capitalists and function in between the exploiters and exploited. In reality they belong to the proletariate but betray their class interest in lieu of the money and patronage they receive from the capitalists.

The novel has been written in the background of a sugar factory and the class struggle which commended in the factory between the labourers and their employers. The different characters of the novel are the representatives of either of the two classes.

Important Character and their classification

1. *Raju.* The character of Raju, as potrayed by the author, reveals the nature and characteristics of the capitalists. In other words Raju represents the capitalist class.

Raju is the son of a rich man and consequently the atmosphere in which he is reared up causes the growth of all characteristics of a capitalist in him. He is materialistic in his outlook as well as very much conscious about his class affiliation. As a man Raju is extremely selfish and unmindful about the problems of poor. He had promised to his poor friend Dallu with a job in his factory but he could not keep his promise and went to Kashmir with a hired girl for enjoyment. Ethical sense of Raju is weak and he is motivated chiefly by the prospect of self satisfaction as well as the satisfaction of instinctive desires.

2. *Sardar Singh.* He is the Manager of a sugar factory and represents the class of middle men. The most significant characteristic of his personality is the enjoyment of worldly pleasures and satisfaction of instinctive desires. He is a very faithful servant of the capitalist though his position is intermediary between the capitalist and the labourers employed in this factory. He is very much particular about safeguarding the interest of the employer and quite frequently employ his hired miscreants to suppress the demand of the poor labourers. In an extreme case he also gets a man murdered who organised the labourers against the employer. He is cruel and unscrupulous Instead of looking at the interest and welfare of the labourers he often exploits them. In other words he betrays his own class identifies with the class of capitalists.

3. *Dallu* He is a poor man and represents the class of the proletariat. Through his character the author has made it clear that the poor people are consistently exploited by the rich and the economic hardship or poverty leads to many unpleasant consequences in their lives. Due to sheer poverty Dallu could not marry the girl whom he loved and ultimately died with his unfulfilled dreams. Dallu's character reminds us of the numerous deprivations and frustrations in a poorman's life.

4. *Lily.* She also represents the class to which Dallu belongs viz. the poor class of people. Her life is also full of tragic events. Her marriage with Dallu fails to materialize because of unfavourable economic conditions. She loves Dallu sincerely. Through the character of Lily the author has acquainted the reader with the sacrifies the worren of the poor homes are to make.

The specific Marxist concept in the Novel

The theme of the novel is based on the Marxian concept of class struggle. It deals with the problems of the poor people. The author has stressed up on the prevailing frustrations and consequent degenaration amongt the poor people caused due to their unsatisfactory economic condition. The economic factor is an effective determinant of the various factors of life and in the absence of a satisfactory economic condition various emotions of the individual viz. love etc. do not develop in a congenial manner. The author is of the opinion that the economic upliftment can change the destiny of the poor mass people. The author has also given a realistic picture of the exploitation of the poor section of the society by the rich. He has patrayed a grim picture of the labourers and workers employed in a sugar factory. Such factories operate in a particular season of the year and as such the workers and labourers are recruited for that period only i.e. for five months. For another seven months in a year they are to find out some other empolyment or to remain idle. This state of affair affects their economic condition adversely. This system of seasonal employment needs change in order to save the labourers from hardship.

The authar has mentioned about the middlemen and described their role. These people are appointed mostly as white collar workers in the factories viz. administrators, managers etc. and take the advantages of their status. They often become instrumental in exploitation of the labourers and workers to the advantages of the capitalists or the employers. They are the agents of the capitalists and also their hand maids.

The author has also pointed out to the necessity of the unity among the proletariat. The workers should unite to protect themselves from the exploitations of the capitalists.

Lastly, the author mentioned about the lavish way of living of the people belonging to the upper class. This is possible due to profit which they earn and accumulate by depriving the labourers of their legitimate remuneration.'

Some Statements consistent with Marxian ideology contained in the Novel

1. 'You are not suppose to love because you are poor... how can you afford sleep when you are hungry? One can not sleep only on sweet words. A child sleeps not only because of the song which the mother sings but the drops of milk pouring into his mouth makes him asleep.

2. 'It was not a marriage rather an auction of some valuable commodities. The rich people treat every place of negotiation as trade centres. They think only of profit and this is the only determining factor or the price of the settlement of negotiation.

......These marriages are unique. When the future generation will think of these people, they will treat these people also as something unique.

3. 'He was an employee in the sugar factory which generally functions for only four to five months in a year. In other words the factory is alive and takes its breath for the limited period it functions. When the factory stops breathing, he also, like hundreds of other labourers, stops breathing.'

4. 'There is no question of giving bonous to the labourers. These pepole unnecessarily want to stop our works......be confident, I will face the challenge. I have seen many strikes in my life. These wretched persons want to exploit us. You need not give them any lift. These are insects. Don't encourage them.

5. 'These farmers are also unique creatures. They have been offered double the price for their lands but they treat their lands as their mothers'.

2. *K.A. Abbas, 'Char Dil Char Ranen'*

The Theme of the Novel

The theme of the novel is based on the Marxist concept of class struggle. The author has described the pathetic condition of the people living within a society based on inequality, injustice and exploitation. He has analysed the various factors responsible for exploitation of the common people. The word 'Char Rahen' (four ways or roads) used by the author as a part of the title of the book suggests the life of the people belonging to the different strata of the society characterised by exploitation, monetary inequality and also the inequality of social status. He, of course, indirectly means the contemporary Indian society within which the people are differentiated on the basis of caste, religion, economic conditions as well as social status. A man belonging to a lower caste cannot marry a girls of a higher caste and vice versa. The women belonging to the poor homes are often acting as the tools for sexual satisfaction of the rich people. The later dominates over them only due to the money which they have been able to accumulate. The inequality as well as the absence of fair mindedness in society often lead to the oppression of the weaker section of the population and more frequently the women. In our society this is very much true that a widow is not allowed to remarry and to lead her entire life in sorrow, deprivation and frustration. She also sometimes become victim of lust and other forms of exploitations. The absence of education makes such widows and women in general more dependent on the males for their subsistence and the males in their turn impose all possible restrictions over them and also consider them as commodities under their exclusive possession. The emphasis on chastity and fidelity on the part of the female is an outcome of the sense of male possessiveness and jealousy. If a women is compelled to loose her virtue under circumstances beyond her control, she is considered as a fallen woman and an object of criticism as well as oppression. She is not given any chance to improve herself. This is why a woman once enters into the life of prostitutes is never allowed, inspite of her sincere desires, to lead a normal life.

The author has, however, given an idea about the society which is surely to emerge in future. The description which he has given about the future society is very much in harmony with the Marxian concept of a classless society. In such a society the working class will unite and form strong trade unions to fight with the capitalists. The united strength of the working class will ultimately make the society free from exploitation.

Important Character and their Classification

1. *Nawbab Rayaset Sultan Abad.* He represents the class of feudal lords or aristrocrats—the predecessors of the capitalists. The persons belonging to this class in our country, have lost their economic superiority with the abolition of zamindary system after the independence and introduction of a new economy very much akin to capitalism. The loss of economic status is naturally followed by the diminition in social status but the persons belonging to the feudal aristrocracy still maintains a vain sense of dignity. They always feel themselves as superior to common men and tries to remain at a distance from them. In other words the author has pointed out that the feudal aristrocracy in consistency with the economy of that stage i.e. feudal economy have developed an outlook as well as bent of mind which is far from being dynamic. The dynamic economy and the open class structure which accompany the capitalism make the adjustment of these die-hards very difficult. Failure of adjustment leads to the gradual extinction of this class from the society. They do not appreciate the social mobility and as a representative of this class Rayasat Sultan Abad is shocked to learn that a 'baniya' of his village has become a cabinet minister. He feels extremely small when he is forced to welcome the person and to pay respect to him.

2. *Joseph Frandex Fera.* He represents the class of employers and exploiters or in other words the Bourgeoisie a necessary growth of capitalist economy. Frandex has been characterised by the author as a hotel keeper employing poor people as servants and extracting inhuman labour from them.

In lieu of that he used to pay them very little. The author has pointed out, quite in consistency with the Marxian concept, that the unpaid labour of the workmen becomes the profit or capitalist. Frandex is very much profit conscious and measures every thing in monetary terms. He is greedy and unscrupulous and does not hesitate even to exploit poor women as call-girls in his hotel. He is also dishonest in his profession and sells illicit liquor to his customers. He rationalizes all his nafarious acts on the ground of earning profit.

3, *Sampuran Singh.* Another representative of the capitalist class—by profession a contractor. He deprives the workers, under his employment, of their legitimate money and also exploited sexually the women labourers. He is greedy, shrewd and unethical. He makes no distinction between virtue and vice in the matters relating to earning money. He is fully aware of the purchasing power of money and believes that any thing in this world can be purchased in lieu of money.

4. *Nirmal Babu.* A marxist in temperament and opposed to all sorts of exploitations. He is a good friend and sympethiser of the proletariat both in urban and rural areas. He has a good standing among the poor people and organises them as well as tries to make them conscious about economic and political realities. He believes in equality and individual freedom. Due to his sincere efforts the workers employed by Sampuran Singh unite and compel the contractor to provide all necessary facilities to them.

5. *Chaveli.* A woman belonging to a poor family. Lust for money motivates her father to marry her with a man of old age but monetarily quite sound. Naturally, she becomes widow at her young age. She is not allowed to marry the young man she loves because of caste barrier. Poverty forces her to leave her village home and join Sampuran's firm as a labourer. The later tries to exploit her sexually and gives her various inducements. She, however, does not succumb and raises her voice against the exploiters. This creates unity among the labourers and they go on strike. Before the united force of the labourers or proletariat the exploitors or the capitalist comes to his knees.

6. *Jhony.* He belongs to a poor fisherman family of South India. Through his character the author has made it clear that no change other than the change in economic conditions in the life of a man can bring any change in his social status. Jhony, previously a Hindu, embraces Christianity with a fealing that Christianity is more liberal as a religion and does not make distinction among its followers. But inspite of his acceptance of Christian ethics, which is more European in character, as well as the foreign dresses viz. trousers etc. his social status remains the same. Poverty compels him to accept an undesirable mode of living and ultimately he accepts a job under Frandex, the hotel keeper. He is exploited by the later and ultimately goes to jail because of raising protest against Frandex. When he finds out that Frandex is using his beloved Sita as a call-girl in his hotel to earn money. The poor man's voice is gaged by the rich whenever it spells out any protest.

The specific Marxist concept in the Novel

1. The concept of class struggle forms the dominant theme of the novel. The concept of class struggle is one of the significant aspect of Marxian ideology and the author as a believer in Marxian ideology—has shown that the struggle among the different classes within a society is caused by the economic reasons. Moreover, the social status of person or group is dependent on the economic position or wealth. No other factor can bring any change in the social status. The author has discared the idea of religious transformation or conversion to more liberal religious faith as an effective means for bringing a sense of equality within the society. He has given the example of such Hudus belonging to lower castes and also economically backward who tried to elevate their social status by changing their religion. They were converted to Christianity but in fact the conversion to a more liberal religious faith could in no way help to improve social status because their economic condition remained unchanged. Thus the author, a believer in Marxian doctorine, has pointed out the omnipotence of economic factors so far as the social status is concerned.

2. The author has also discussed the ethics of capitalism which is based on the materialistic concept of life. Money is more important than morality. Accumulation of money is given the maximum impetus in a capitalist society and money at the same time is the only measuring tool used to measure the efficiency of any subject or person. Money, moreover, has the maximum purchasing power and naturally the men of capital think that each and every requirements of life can be obtained in lieu of money. Morality chastity, honesty all are outdated concepts in a capitalist society and the success of a man's life is judged by the amount of money he is able to accumulate either by fair or foul means.

3. The author has also described the growing awareness among the younger generations in a capitalist society like one found in our land against the exploitation of the labourers by the capitalist employers and their agents. The modern society is gradually drifting nearer to socialism and the entire weaker and at the same time exploited section of the mass is uniting by amalgamation of their respective class interests against the tyrannies of the capitalists. The trade unions are being organised with a view to safeguard the interests of the workers.

4. Finally, the author has mentioned about the decay of feudalism in India as a part of historical realism to pave the way for the capitalism to come in. The forces of democracy and socialism have also made their appearances in the society. This is accompanied by various changes within the society. In case of the individuals the new forces have amancipated them from numerous boundages and a sense of individualism has started developing. The former society with closed classes has been forced to accommodate the modern forces and as a result the closed class structure is being replaced by the open class system. This phenomenon in its own turn has increased the 'life chances' for the people and also accelarated the social mobility.

Some statements consistent with Marxian ideology contained in the Novel

1. "Socialism is the way of salvation. Socialism is the only alternative which can provide to every man the very necessities

of life i.e. bread, cloth, shelter, education, culture, peace, progress etc."

2. "Chaveli : it will be a new road where there will be no contractor. Every body will work collectively. The Government have given contract to the labourer's Cooperative Society to construct the road.

3. "Listen to me with attention. The law of our country says that no employer can force his employees to work for morel than eight hours in a day. The same law will also be implemented in your firm. No worker will work for more than eight hours. Secondly the wage will be one rupee per day. Thirdly you will take steps to repair these huts of the labourers and finally, you will give them facilities of light and water."

4. "Do you know that those days are coming when the distinction of caste will no more exist.

5. "What do you talk about marriage ? Every night I celebrate new marriage. Take these ten rupees. From tomrrow I will depute you to a place where you will have to work less and that way you will enjoy it."

6. "I always used to think that why there is distinction in this world ? Why Radha is Brahmin ? Why Govinda is an Aheer and myself an untouchable Chama ? It is true that God has created such differences. Some people are placed in higher position and they are at the top."

7. "Do you know who was the father of this minister ? He was an ordinary shopkeeper. The minister himself was an ordinary pleader when he went to the jail with Gandhi. After he came back from jail he started a shop selling handloom products. I had to go to the station to pay my respects, to him. Instead of visiting my place he had asked me to come where he was staying. You can understand that the son of a Nawab, Sir Azimuddolah, who ruled over the state in the tenth generation had to pay respects to that son of an ordinary Baniya."

8. "When our parent were converted into Christianity, the priests told them that henceforth they would not be differentiated from other Christians whatever might be their economic status. All of them were equal because they were the sons of Almighty the God. But after conversion the

distinction remained. The upper caste Hindu maintained the same attitude of indifference which they did maintain with the lower caste people. The white Christians also never tolerated the black Christians. Once my grand father went to the Church but he was not allowed to enter."

3. *Krishan Chander, 'Jab-Khet-Jage'*

The theme of the Novel

The theme of the novel is based on the peasant movement of Telengana in South India and the decay of the feudal lord of Sri Rampur, a village in the same district. The story describes the struggle between the 'haves' and 'havenots', a typical concept of Marxian thesis. The author has given a vivid description of the exploitation of the 'wittis' by the fedual lord who used to live in a big house under the protection of armed guards and he had no time to think about the subjects who lived virtually like animals. He ignored completely the rights of his 'Wittis' or subjects, and forced them to work in his fields without paying any remuneration. That state of affair, however, started changing when the communists and another political party named Andhra Mahasabha, leftist organisation, started their agitation against the exploitation of the feudal lord and demanded the legitimate rights of the tillers and poor labourers. The accumulated hatred in the minds of the people belonging to the later sections for centuries towards the feudal lords helped them to unite and fight for their rights as well as emancipation from the tyrranies and exploitations. Soon after the movement took a violent form and the exploiters of the neighbouring areas also organised themselves and tried to protect the feudal lord of Sri Rampur. The army of Nizam and also the Razakars, a volunteer force of the exploiters, attacked the village in order to foil the movement of the poor and exploited people. But, as the Marxists claims, even the superior strength of the exploiters could not stand before the combined strength of the exploited people. A large number of people, however, had to give their lives but ultimately they could capture the land belonging to the feudal lord and distribute the same among the poor and landless villagers. The poor people became the master of the land which they were tilling as unpaid labourers. Their happiness knew no bounds.

This, however, was not an isolated event in the village Sri Rampur rather the peasant movement against the feudal lords spread all over Telengana which was named as Andhra Pradesh after the achievement of independence. The movement, moreover, brokeout during the last days of British empire in India when the feudal lords were patronized by the government and Telengana was the part of the domain of the Nizam of Hyderabad, a native ruler as well as a pampered child of the British administrators.

Soon after the completion of the movement India was made independent by the Britishers and Telengana became a part of the Indian union. The hoisting of the tricolour flag, the symbol of the independent and unified India created new hopes in the minds of the people all over and particularly Telengana. They naturally expected that in the changed setup that reactionary force will not be able to attempt for the restoration of the old order which according to Marx is a characteristic of the struggle between bourgeois and the proletariat. The people of Telengana also became happy when the Indian army for the first time entered into the region and gave them a hearty reception. They considered the Indian army as the force supporting the cause of the liberated mass and protesting their rights.

Their expectations, however, were proved otherwise soon after the formation of the congress ministry in the newly created Andhra Pradesh on August 15, 1947. The new government proclaimed their intention to persue the principle of non-violence and promote democratic values but quite contrary to their proclamation and expectations of the people, soon made a compromise with the reactionary elements viz. the Nizam and the other feudal lords of the region. An order was issued challenging the legality of the land occupied by the villagers and at the same time directing them to return all such land to their former occupants. In case of non-compliance of the order the occupants of such lands were threatened to be dealt with as criminals.

A wave of discontent and consequently violence broke out as the reaction against the order. Fighting broke out and large number of peasants and poor workers were arrested. Few of them were also given death sentence because they took arms against the government which was an act of treason in the eyes of the law of the land.

The author has pointed out the reactionary nature of the newly formed government headed by bourgeois politicians. Such a government quite naturally endeavour to protect the interest of the feudal aristrocracy and all other reactionary forces.

The author has also criticised the feudal society for its shortcomings and particularly the exploitation of the poor by the rich feudal lords. He has also revealed the changes that take place in the structure of opinion as well as motivation of the common people as a result of the impact of Marxist ideology or communism, in other words.

The story of the novel is not only Raghu Rao, a twenty years old farmer but it is at the same time an account of the class struggle in rural areas between the exploiters and the exploited.

Raghu Rao represents the new generation of peasants who are quite conscious of the injustice done to them and also about their rights. They are quite aware of the fact that no amount of persuation nor any charismatic element like fate etc. can bring any change in their existing status. The only wayout lies in the united strength of the proletariat class. The class war in enevitable and in this struggle the proletariat always comes out victorious over the bourgeois exploiters.

Important characters and their classification

1. *Raghu Rao.* He was a poor farmer of a village named Sri Rampur of Telengana in South India. He was born in a family which was extremely poor and since his childhood he was acquainted with poverty and exploitation of the poor people by rich feudal lords. The poor peasants could never think of the fulfilment of the bare necessities of life. Raghu

Rao could learn, at his early age, that the son of a feudal lord could easily seduce a girl of the poor family and no body could oppose that. He had left the village and went to the city. The city was not free from exploitation but the nature of the exploitation was different than that of the rural area. In the city he came in contact with Maqbool, a communist leader and learnt about the ideology of Marx. He also learnt to read and write. He could develop the belief that the misfortune of the poor can be removed only by means of struggle, if required even violent, with the exploiters.

After he came back to his village the peasants and poor labourers organised under his leadership and he initiated the violent movement of the united proletariat against the land lord of the village. The victory of the proletariat was followed by the distribution of occupied lands of the land lord among the poor people and peasants. He also started educational institution in his village and organised the societies of women and farmers. When the reactionary forces attempted for the restoration of former order and the army of Nizam as well as Razakars attacked the village he fought like a brave general. Ultimately he was arrested and sentenced to death. He accepted the sentence with a smile on his lips.

Raghu Rao, therefore, represents the class of exploited people in the rural areas of our country. He is also the symbol of the new generation of young men who having been enlightened by the ideology of Marx, do not hesitate to wage war against the exploiters. They are non believers in super—natural or supra mental. Their approach is very much objective and they believe that class. Struggle is the inevitable measure which can bring emancipation of the exploited people of the world. Such a young people are the organisers, social workers and martyrs for the cause of poor and exploited mass.

2. *Viraiya* : The character of Viraiya represents the class of oppressed people in the society, heavily laden with poverty and almost incapable of expressing any sense of resentment to exploiters or wrong doers. They harbor deep sense of hatred towards the class of bourgeoisie and sense of frustration caused due to severe deprivation in all the spheres of life. These feeelings are transferred from one generation to the other.

In the novel we find Viraiya as the father of Raghu Rao, the principal character of the story. He was a poor farmer without having any title over the land he used to cultivate. He was practically a slave of the land lord and whenever called by the later he went with folded hands and a sense of awe in his mind. He reared his son. Raghu Rao, in the midst of extreme poverty and through him his son could develop a realistic image of the rich people and their behaviour to the poor. He could feel in his early childhood that the poor had no right even to touch the commodities, meant for the rich. Once while he was a child went to a 'mela' with his father Viraiya and out of the curiosity touched a costly cloth which was exibited in a shop. That made the shopkeeper angry and to rebuke him. The incident and the feeling of humiliation created an impression in the minds of Raghu Rao and when his father went to the jail to meet his son before the execution of his death sentence he reminded his father of the incidence and asked him to be steady. The father, an ignorant person, could not, however, understand the implication and thought that his son wanted to wear a silken garment. Like an affectionate father he prepared one such garment in the night and went so the jail with that, alongwith the procession of the farmers and poor labourers of his village.

The author through this pathetic incident wants, probably, to remind his readers that irrespective of the economic condition all men have the same set of instinctive and emotional qualities. The man made distinction of economic classes makes it difficult in case of the people belonging to the lower economic classes to cultivate these qualities in a healthy manner. The classless society with equitable distribution of wealth will ensure an atmosphere quite congenial for all men to express their instinctive and emotional qualities in a healthy way.

3. *Chundri* : A poor gipsy girl. Her character in the novel reminds the readers of the exploitation which the young and beautiful girls of the poor homes has to suffer in the hands of the rich men with voluptuous character. The later treat the girls as commodities and do not care for any sentimental

or emotional prerequisite in case of sexual intercourse either for themselves or for the girls.

Chundri a beautiful young girl of the village Sri Rampur was summoned by the land lord of the village, Pratap Narain Reddy, for sexual intercourse and the girl had to succumb before the evil design of that rich men. She was exploited because she was helpless.

The land lord treated Chundri as a commodity and therefore he had a right over her as he had the right over all other commodities within his estate. The poor girl loved Raghu Rao but all her hopes of union with the man he loved were foiled after she had to surrender before the zamindar. Her tribes men also could not dare to resist because they had to depend for their subsistence on the zamindar, Paratap Narain Reddy.

4. *Maqbool* : He represents the class of young men who having drawn the inspiration from the Marxian ideology want to change the society in a manner which will put an end to all forms of exploitations and oppressions.

Maqbool was a staunch follower of Marxian ideology and also indoctrinated Raghu Rao. It is due to his inspiration that Ragbu Rao could initiate a peasant revolt againt the feudal lord of his village. Maqbool like a true Marxist did not believe in the distinction created among men by means of caste, religion etc. He believed that the only real demarcation in the society exists on the basis of economic gradations of the people. He also believed that for the good of the mankind and restoration of human dignity the society must be 'classless' and the wealth must be distributed in an equitable manner.

The specific Marxist concept in the Novel

1. The novel is based on the concept of class struggle as given by Karl Marx i.e. the history of all the hitherto existing society is the history of class struggle. The story of the novel is an account of the conflict between the zamindars and the poor peasants. The former represent the exploiters and the later represent the exploited classes in the society.

2. Secondly, the author has indicated, quite consistently with Marxian theory that the united strength of the proletariat is sure to defeat the forces of the bourgeoisie, in spite of the superior striking power of the later. In other words the author has supported the Marxian claim that the days of exploitation can be removed from the society only when proletariat unite.

3. Thirdly, the author tells us like a true believer in Marxian ideology that the bourgeois reactionaries after their defeat try once more to stage a 'come back'. In this attempt they try to exploit the religious sentiment of the people and more particularly the communal sentiment.

4. Fourthly, the author explains that no country can be liberated in true sense unless the proletarian forces get a firm grip over the administration. The government led by the middle class bourgeoisie or reactionaries, (the newly formed congress government in Andhra Pradesh after the independence of India in 1947), according to the author, betray the interest of the poor peasants and workers. Such a government invariably side with the reactionaries and exploiters of the former days.

5. Fifthly, the author has said that the real owner of the land is he who cultivates it. Moreover, if the peasants revolt and establish their right over the land they plough as well distribute the land in possession of the land lord in an equitable manner they can not be treated as usurpers rather the landlords or the zamindars should be held responsible for occupying the lands belonging to the peasants for centuries.

6. Sixthly, the author has pointed out the tendency of commoditization of all the object even human life in the feudal as well as capitalist societies. Everything is measured in terms of money and the rich man claims that every thing is available in lieu of money.

7. Seventhly, the author has claimed that the distinctions which exist among the different grades of human beings on the basis of religion, caste, race etc. are unreal. The distinction is based on the economic status of the people.

8. Eighthly, the author has tried to introduce his readers to a class of people in younger generation those who believe that class struggle is inevitable, classless society is possible,

the proletariat must unite, and the wealth should be distributed equitaby—in other words this band of young Marxist are very much optimistic about the end of the present order i.e. capitalism, and the approach of a new era free from exploitation, indignity and frustration.

9. Ninethly, the author has revealed the selfish tendencies of the zamindars. They never appreciated any enlightenment of their subjects. They considered the education for the poor people or peasants as useless. They were rather afraid of educationg them because they believed that education would put new ideas into their minds or might sow the seeds of revolution. They wanted their subjeets to remain as the bullocks tied with the oil pressure i.e. they would work without any grumbling—like a machine.

10. Tenthly, the author has exposed the accumulated hatred in the hearts of the poor people against their exploiters the rich people and the landlords. This hatred is transferred from one generation to the other in a process of inheritance.

11. Lastly, we get numerous instances in the novel of the exploitation, injustice indignity and frustration which the poor labourers and peasants had to face in the hands of the lords and their hired agents.

Some statements consistent with Marxian ideology contained in the novel

1. 'The son of a Witti is a Witti as the son of a zamindar is a zamindar, the son of a Nambardar is Nambardar and the son of a priest is a priest'.

2. 'We are Witti, we are the slaves of the zamindars. Whenever he will call us we will go to him'.

3. 'Don't you know that no body can wear a new dress when he goes to meet his zamindar'.

4. 'My son, the owner of the Banku (building) is our enemy. My son, this hatred I have inherited from my father. Now you have grown up and you will inherit the hatred from me. People generally give some property to their sons but I have no property. I have only this hatred and I will transfer it to you'.

5. 'Nageshwar asked Raghu Rao about Mascow. He did not know what it is. Raghu Rao told him that *Mascow* is a city but at the same time an ideology'.

6. 'Profit and exploitation has nothing to do with religion. It is the tradition of our country that whenever the vested interest and the reactionaries are defeated they take the help of the communal forces'.

7. 'This incidence of our village is not a new one. Whenever the farmer refuse to give the share to the Jagirdars or Desmukhs such incidence and even more serious happen. In the past their forces had attacked the village in the darkness of night, set on fire to the house and went away'.

8. 'In fact the land belongs to those who labour on it'.

9. 'Zamindar used to think that education even reading and writing, was not necessary for common people. Spread of edcation would lead to revolution by creating new ideas in the minds of the people.

The peasant or kisan who was like a bullock lied with oil pressure might have considered himself as a human being. The zamindars required bullocks and not human beings.'

10. 'The real owner of the land is one who ploughs it and toils over it. How can it belong to those who build their palaces on others' income and abuse us. The leaders of the congress party tell the peasants of Andhra to return the land to the zamindars. But why not the congress ask the zamindars who have occupied our land for centuries ?

11. 'If the resistance to exploitation is violence; the defence of our lives is violence; protection given to our mothers and other women folk is violence; safeguarding the golden crop produced in the fields of the village is violence; then to remain alive is a violence; to take our breath is violence, and the palpitation of heart is also violence.

12. 'Look here the entire Telengana will lead the procession of the winners. Capture the target. O'sons of Andhra Come Up'.

4. *Razia Sajjad Zaheer, 'Suman'*

The theme of the Novel

The theme of the novel is based on the inner conflict within our society and explains the gradual emergence of the communist ideology in the urban setting of India after the partition of the country. The novelist traces the gradual shift from the old values of Indian society to the new ideologies of humanism and socialism. She stresses upon the changing status and role of women in our society. With the achievement of independence Indian Society experienced a new wave of changes and beginning of the new progressive movement under the banner of communism. The new trends paved the way for the gradual emergence of the society in which the weaker section came forward and get ready to participate in the class struggle.

The novel throws light upon a society through the characters of Rafique Sahib, Yusuf and Suleman who wanted to change the old pattern of the society and opposed any form of exploitation of the weaker section by the stronger or wealthy section.

Suman was the daughter of a prostitute but she was very much inspired by the writings of the different progressive writers who had written powerful articles against the immoral traffic in women. She also came to know about such homes which provided protection and shelter to those prostitutes who wanted to leave the profession and lead a respectable life. Suman was one such girl who wanted to come out of the vicious life and in her mission she solicited the cooperation of Rafique Sahib and Yusuf. To other characters of the novel viz. Javed and Shadi Lal are the models of bourgeois exploiters. Both of them used to exploit the poorer section of the people to fulfil their personal interests. Javed for instance could take the advantage of the poverty of a poor maid servant and satisfied his sexual lust but on the other hand, wanted to marry another woman only because she was the daughter of a rich man. Likewise, Shadi Lalji did not hesitate to force the poor girls of the Ashram, of which he was the secretary, to go to bed with other people and that way earned money or get the patronage of the influencial people as well as the bureaucrats.

The inner contradiction within our society has clearly been exposed by the authoress and she is obviously influenced by the Marxian ideology. Quite consistent to Marxian ideology she advocates that the proletariat should come forward and unite themselves to remove the disparity between the 'haves' and 'have-nots'.

About the prostitutes the authoress feels that they are a class of exploited women and the profession of prostitution, she considers, as the outcome of poverty as well as some other social factors.

Important characters and their classification

Suman : The heroine of the novel. She was born and brought up in a prostitute family. Through her character the authoress has endeavoured to expose the existence of the exploiters and their agents within the society who foil most of the measures adopted for the improvement of the poor and weaker section of the people.

Suman, although a daughter of a prostitute, was given proper education as well as lesson in fine arts viz. music and dance. The healthy orientation, naturally, created a craving within her to come out of the vicious life of a prostitute and to lead a life of respect and digasnity. Education could enlarge her mental arena and she became more inclined to Marxian ideology which stand against and also suggests way for the removal of the disparity and exploitation from the society. She felt elated when she could come to know about the homes for destitute and fallen women. These homes were meant for protecting such women and help them to lead a dignified life.

Suman, with all expectations joined such a home but it did not take a long time for her illusion to be removed. She could know that in spite of the sincere efforts made by the authorities they are not able to protect the women from the intrigues of the rich and influencial people who earn money from the tradea of flesh. In many cases the secretaries of such homes are no better than the pimps. Out of disgust she left the rescue home and could start a dignified life with the cooperation of two well meaning persons viz. Rafique Sahib and Javed.

2. *Rafique Sahib* : He represents the class of intelligensia with a liberal outlook and inclination to give lead to the common people in order to make them concious about the inequalities prevailing within the society and also to fight against it. By profession Rafique was a Professor of English literature and at the same time a staunch supporter of Communist movement in India. He could organise a group consisting of progressive writers and also made sincere efforts to create consciousness among the poor and exploited sections of people regarding social inequality and the necessity of class struggle. The character of Rafique Sahib reminds us of such people who dedicate their lives for the cause of the poor people and staunchly follow the ideology which they think to be correct and effectiveness.

3. *Yusuf* : He belonged to a middle class family. He was inspired by the desire for social reconstruction and became a follower of the communist ideology. His dedication to the cause of the poor also led to suffering and personal loss. In spite of his high academic qualification he was forced to accept a petty job because his inclination towards the left ideology was a disqualification to get a good job in a society controlled by the right reactionaries.

Yusuf, however, believed that classless society is possible and that will put an end to all exploitations and disparities within the society. His character reminds the readers of the fact that ultimate triumph of the people lies in dedicated and selfless efforts.

4. *Neelam & Sohni* : They represent the class of women who are exploited either because of their poverty or due to the various taboos prevailing within the society which give an edge to the male over the female. The poor girls are often forced to sleep with people who pay them money and satisfy their lust. In other cases the girls also fall victims of

unscrupulous people who make them pregnant and do not marry. Such girls, in an orthodox society like ours, are compelled to lead the life of prostitutes. Neelam belonged to the first and Sohni to the second. Both were exploited by a rich debauch.

5. *Javed* : Represents the class of rich people or the exploiters, according to Marx. His motive was to earn more money and pastime was to play with the virginity as well as sentiments of girls and also to indulge in drinking. Every act was fair, according to his ethics, if that helped him to fetch more money. He was an extremely selfish man with materialistic outlook and had least regard for the finer sentiments or ethical values. He was a capitalist.

The specific Marxist concept in the Novel

The characters of the novel are the clear indications of the impact of Marxian ideology on the story as well as the authoress. The authoress has explained the capitalist social order with the materialistic way of life which developed on the ruins of feudalism. The capitalistic social order has its own code of conduct and structure of motives which differ from the previous one dominated by moral values and religious motivation. The product of the capitalist society is identified in the character of Javed. He is a man with materialistic outlook, matter of fact approach and a strong inclination towards accumulation of money. He believed more on the utility and power of money than in the observance of ethical code of conduct. Moreover, he considered nothing as unfair in earning or accumulation of money.

Secondly, the authoress believes and she is hopeful that the spread of Marxian ideology will make the way clear for the emergence of a social order based on the concept of human dignity, individual freedom and quality of opportunities. The authoress has also traced the changes those we find have occurred in our society during the post Independence period. In spite of the barriers created by the reactionaries and the capitalist society has drifted, at least to a little extent, towards the desired goal. New expectations about the future and the consciousness about the maladies of the present as well as the tendency for a concerted action against the exploiters have started developing. All these have become possible, as the authoress feels, due to the spread of Marxian ideology in this country in the post Independence period. Thirdly, the authoress points out that with a change in the social order the pattern of human relationship also undergo modifications. In the capitalist society, for example, the relationship is determined more by economic factors than such determinants like blood, kinship, birth etc. Moreover, when one tries to start some social relationship with another, say for example marriage, he is more guide by economic considerations than any other viz. family tradition, character, disposition etc. Finer sentiments like love, affection etc. are not treated as much significant. Apart from this the relationships are generally confined within the limits of the economic gradation to which the person belongs. This means the people in a capitalist society becomes more class conscious than in any other form.

Fourthly, the authoress has rejected the idea of the predetermined status or in other words status determined by birth or the inequality of sexes as a natural phenomenon. Rather she has pointed out to the changing role of women in our contemporary society and pleaded to end all sorts of exploitations of the women by men.

Lastly, in order to expose the grave consequences of social maladies the authoress has claimed that prostitution as a social institution developed as a result of the injustice which was prevailing in feudal society and the accommodation of the same in the capitalist social order is the cause for its sustenance. She has suggested various measures to eradicate the prostitution from the society and has stressed upon the spread of female education as well as equality of sexes.

Some statements consistent with Marxian ideology contained in the novel

(1) 'The Labour class in the contemporary society can not survive without the formation of a strong organisation of themselves'.

2. 'The backwardness of the society can not be removed unless every individual within the society is given a guarantee for his employment as well as equal opportunity'.

3. 'Communists want equality and justice all over the world. They hate those who lack compassion for the poor and admire those who love the poor people. I have heard that in the countries rules by the communists there is no prostitution and the women are free, happy and permitted to do any work of which they are capable. They are not the parasites of the males and have full freedom in selecting partners of their own choices'.

4. 'Nafis is almost similar to the other girls of rich parents. For them literature is a fashion, politics is a pastime, poets and writers are the articles of decoration just like the toys made either of the paper of Bengal, clay of Lucknow, or wood of Benaras. They give pure milk to their pet-dogs and take whisky for recreation'.

5. 'The rich people can not realise the significance of love. It is a commodity which can not be purchased in lieu of money and the rich people have no understanding about such thing which can not be bought or sold'.

6. 'Suman! never trust a rich man Whatever he may look like but he is always conscious of the wealth he possesses'.

7. '...Now we shall take active part in the development of the country. Mere criticism is not enough, we also require the participation of the people in the programme of reconstruction. Only those who have participated can criticise. If there is a leackage in the dam, we have no right to criticise because in case we would have taken part in the construction there would not have been any leakage in the dam'.

8. 'The total environment of the house was adverse to the mental make-up of Yusuf. They had a strong attachment with wealth, and every thing was measured in terms of money !

9. '...Between you and Yusuf such a man intends to enter who has no regard for your sentiments. He is more interested in your wealth. He is a smuggler and now he is trying to earn lakhs of rupees by obtaining a licence through the influence

of your father. He supplies even wine and women to high officials to get his works done'.

5. *Kalsm Urfi, 'Gham Khan-e-Dil'*

The theme of the Novel

The author, Kalim Urfi has tried to draw the attention of his readers to the inability of the present government of the country in solving the various social problems viz poverty, unemployment, exploitation of the weaker and poorer section of the people by the stronger and rich people etc. The mode of the production and distribution of wealth is determined in our society by the class of capitalists and this phenomenon inevitably leads to class differentiation on the basis of accumulated wealth or capital. The character of Javed introduces the readers to the problem of educated unemployment among the middle as well as poor class of people. Hundred .and thousands of Javeds enter into the university campus with much of hopes and aspirations but their hopes turn into hallucinations when they come out of the campus and start searching a job suited to their qualifications.

The parents of such young people also feel equally frustrated because in most of the cases they meet the expenses of the higher education with much hardship and it will neither be an exaggeration nor untrue to say that in some cases the mother has to sell her ornaments to meet the expenses of the higher education of her children. They bear the hardship with a hope that the son after being educated may bring the days of happiness and comforts in the family. When their hopes are shattered they naturally feel extremely miserable.

The author has also drawn the picture of the rich or affluent class of people within the society. They are known to the common people as capitalists. Those people live in plenty and do not feel the paucity of any commodity of consumption. The young men belonging to this class need not be crazy about employment and they can afford to idle awey their times as well as indulge dancing, drinking, gambling and other such expensive vices.

As a remedy to this situation the author has mentioned about the effectiveness of class war. He is also of the opinion that the Red revolution may put an end to the present chaos and crisis. He feels that a day will come when the poorer section of the people will fight unto the last in order to bring changes in the government as well as society. He is of the view that the class differentiation in our contemporary society can be removed only by introducing communism. The ideology of Marx can make the society free from all sorts of exploitations. The author has stressed upon the fact that the wealth as well as poverty belong to all and as such they should be distributed in an equitable manner, irrespective of the caste, creed, colour, religion and sex. The author points out to a society free from restrictions, limitations as well as tyranny and exploitations.

Important characters and their classification

Javed : Belonged to a middle class family with meager income. After passing his bachelor's examination he tried his best to get a job suited to his qualification. But he was unsuccessful in his attempts. This caused the development of a feeling of frustration and sense of disappointment in his mind and also made him antagonistic to the government as well as the contemporary set up which could not create sufficient avenues of employment in order to accommodate the job seekers.

His character, as created by the author, reminds the reader of the importance of economic factor in all spheres of human life, includinj the conjugal life. Javed married Khalda—beautiful girl, but he could not be happy in his conjugal life. He was unable to provide even the bare necessities of life to his beloved wife. The mental agony and the physical impoverishment ultimately led him to suffer from tuberculosis. He died a premature death and left behind his wife, mother and two young unmarried sisters.

Javed's character is an indicator of the maladies which exist in our contemporary society and also tells us about the mental frustration and material deprivation which the majority of the people belonging to middle and poor classes are to bear. Like Javed a large number of young educated people learn through their better experiences in lives that the remedy lies in class struggle and the ultimate victory of the 'Have-nots' over the 'haves'. The removal of class differences which has already become quite deep rooted, is possible only by a revolution or class war.

2. *Khalda* : Her character can be described as the tale of a poor girl whose emotion and sentiments were crushed under the heavy pressure of poverty before they actually could attain their full growth. She was married to Javed but the later could not get an employment and was forced to live in the midst of poverty as well as deprivation. The author once again has reminded his readers through the character of Khalda about the omnipotence of economic factors in our lives. He also points out to the fact that the finer sentiments and tender emosions require an atmosphere free from poverty, anxiety and exploitation for their growth. The poor man fails to develop then under unfavourable conditions of life and also due to his preoccupation with the problems of every day life related mostly to the economic or material necessities or wants.

4. *Kazmi* : Belong to an upper class Muslim family. He was an opportunist and a careerist at the same time. He has no consideration for the poor people and their problems. On the other hand he devoted most of his time in seeking pleasure. He enjoyed gossiping and liked to dance in parties. Regdrding wine he was free from any prejudice and had sufficient means to indulge in various costly pastimes. By dint of his social connections and rich family back fround he could, without much toil, establish himself in life and managed to secure an assignment in the foreign service of the country.

The specific Marxist concept in the Novel

Firstly, the author has expressed his belief in quite clear terms that the present chaos and crises in the society are all due to the capitalist form of government. He has also suggested the class struggle as the only remedy for all maladies in the society.

Secondly, the author also believes that the social problems such as poverty, unemployment etc. are all artificial in nature and created by the capitalists. Thirdly, the author also claims that the economic crises lead to unhappy social life.

Fourtaly, the author observes that communism is the only solution of the present chaos and misery of the people. He believes that the message of Karl Marx can remove the class differences which has been created by the vested interest within the society.

Fifthly, the author has pointed out that the ethics of the affluent section or the capitalist class is quite different from the poor section of the people within the society.

Sixthly, the author has spoken about the classless society characterised by the absence of any distinction between individuals on the basis of caste, creed, religion, or sex etc.

Lastly, the author stresses upon the fact that the wealth of a country or society never belongs to any particular class of the people. Every individual irrespective of any distinction has a share in it. It is, therefore, suggested that the wealth should be distributed in an equitable manner.

Some statements consistent with Marxian ideology contained in the Novel

1. 'Capitalism is that type of economic system in which the production of wealth as well as its distribution is concentrated in the hands of few persons. These persons are known as capitalists. The wealth they invest in business is called capital and their rule over the society is termed as capitalist government.'

2. ......After all he was hungry and the pang of hunger developed a habit of reading the Russian and Chinese literature in him. He wanted to make him free from this golden world and its blood sucking government.

3. 'Red revolution is the only remedy of the present chaos. The message of a Jew (Karl Marx) can give relief to the world.

In the absence of this the entire world will be weeping and the chastity of Jhansi-Ki Rani, Marium and Seeta will be sold for few silver coins or few pieces of bread'.

4. 'I will not accept my defeat. I am not begging rather I am demanding my rights. If I am denied my right I will snatch it from others.'

5. 'Hungry people will become conscious of their rights and each hungry person will communicate his feeling of hunger to other such persons. They will raise their voices against the present order which denies them of their legitimate rights.'

6. 'He needed bread for his survival but a handful of persons were in possession of the entire resources of the world and they could erect a golden wall.'

7. 'A man without wealth is not a man in the proper sense of the term. Neither he possesses any ethical value nor the humanitarian qualities Wealth is a great gift.'

8. 'Karl Marx was a great man of Germany. His ideology aimed at the removal of the problems which the human beings use to face. The wealth of the world, he claimed, belonged to all and, therefore, the distribution of wealth should have been equitable.'

9. 'He was waiting for the day when the human beings will fight the decisive war unto the last for the elimination of class distinction.

10. 'While studying about the Russian revolution he used to think whether such a revolution could evercome to India.'

11. 'A man can purchase every thing in exchange of wealth. When wealth can purchase man's mind as well ns conscience then what is left?.'

12. 'The world is more like a chess board and the poor people are the pawns of this board moving at the whims and mercy of the rich people.'

13. 'Why not we establish a society free from limitations, political tyranny, and all sorts of exploitations viz. legal, physical and bureaucratic.'

6

Impact of Freudian Idea on Urdu Novels

The urdu novels in the past several decades were very much influencied by the ideas of three eminent personalities viz. Mohan Das Karamchand Gandhi, Karl Marx and Sigmund Freud. Gandhi's insistence on non-violence as well as on the simplicity and purity of personal life touched ares-ponsive chord in the inherent idealism of Indian thought and thus inspired indirectly the India creative writers. Karl Marx brought a revolution in modern thought through his concept of dialectical materialism which gave a much needed jolt to the traditional way of thinking and attitude. Sigmund Freud is best known for his discovery of unconscious mental life or the 'primary process', as some analystic call it. His ideas have immensely influenced the contemporary literary mind.

Freud exerted a powerful influence not only in the field of psychology and psychiatry but in all fields of knowledge and culture. He broke the traditional ways of thinking and liberated the human spirit to accept new trends of life. Freudian school has been established in different branches of knowledge which were interpreted in the background of Freudian concepts. Urdu literature was also remarkably influenced by the materialistic and psycho-analytical trends which developed in the contemporary European literature as a result of world war-I. A powerful and talented group of writers attempted to start a new age in urdu novels based on the psycho-analytical approach to life and specially the sex-centred life.

Sex in one form or the other has always been the main theme of most fictions but the physical aspect of sex was covered under some kind of spiritual clock and there was no frank approach in describing the sexual affairs of the characters. The fiction writers generally used to describe 'love' as something mysterious but under the influence of Freudian psychology this mysterious concepts of love or sex have been replaced by a frank and free discussion of the physical aspect of sex. As a matter of fact a section of urdu novelists have accepted sex as the chief motivating factor in human activities. These writers depict sex in its fullest exposition instead of the darkness of taboos and under the cover of moral or ethical values. Earlier the urdu novelists talked of about sex in a restricted way and they did not disclose the sexual conducts of their characters. The society was dominated by religions and spiritual values and the writer tried to abide by them. The novelists of that age, for instance, Moulvi Nazir Ahmad, Rashidul Khairi etc. wrote on moral and ethical themes and did not dare to discuss the sexual behaviour or the problems related to the sexual life in the characters of their novels. The impact of Freudian ideas brought, however, a radical change in literary world and the eminent urdu novelists like Aziz Ahmad, Krishan Chander, Ismat Chughtai and many others started writing about the sex centred life of the contemporary society as well as several problems associated with it.

The concept of time as a continuous flow has influenced the literary minds who developed a new kind of narrative texture of plot of novels that moved backward and forward with a freedom to try to capture the sense of time as it actually operates in the human awareness of it. This new concept of time has been derived from the work of Freud and his disciples. The individual's personality is the sum total of the individual's memories. The past exists always in the present, colouring and determining the nature of present response, and to tell the truth about a character's reaction to any situation we must tell the whole truth about everything that has ever happened to him. The novelists who have been influenced by this concept of time and consciousness will seek ways of communicating to the reader the simultaniety of different levels of consciousness and he will also realise that the whole truth about a mature person can be told by probing into his past through presenting the full texture of his present consciousness which resulted in a new kind of fictional technique known as 'stream of consciousness'. It is a means to escape from the tyranny of the time-dimension. It is not only in the distinct memories that the past impinges on the present; but also in much vulgar and more subtle ways, our mind floating off down some channel superficially irrelevant but really having a definite starting off place from the initial situation; so that in presenting the character's reaction to events, the author will show us states of mind being modified by associations and recollections deriving from the present situation but referring to a constantly shifting series of events in the past. As a matter of fact modern writers have realised that a psychologically accurate account of what men is at any given moment can be given neither in terms of a static description of his character nor in terms of a group of chronologically arranged reactions to a series of circumstances. They have become interested in those aspects of consciousness which can be viewed as progression of individual and self existing moments, but which are essentially dynamic rather than static in nature and are independent of the given moment. Novelists who employ the 'Stream of consciousness' treat the character as a process and present it outside time and place in the double sense; first, they separate the presentation of consciousness from the chronological sequence of events, and second, they enable the quality of a given state of mind to be investigated so completely that we do not need to wait for time to make the potential actual before we can see the whole.

This psychological techniques to describe themes in modern novels is the outcome of the Freudian impact on literature. This has also been adopted by the urdu novelists who took it from the English novels. Qurratal Ain Haider's 'Aag Ka Darya' is a very good example of stream of consciousness in urdu novels.

The greatest achievement of Sigmund Freud is the theory of psycho-analysis which studies the unconscious functions of the mind and personality. "It aims at an empirical observation on those determinants of human personality and behaviour which are not disclosed by the investigation of rational thought and motivation (either by introspection or by direct study of another)."[1] By this psychoanalytic technique Freud studied the details of unconscious thoughts, memories and wishes which act as vital factors in the motivation of human behaviour. Every mental act can be shown by the study of their unconscious impulses e.g. phantasy, symptoms, wishes etc, "Unsatisfied wishes, according to Freud, "are the deriving power behind phantasies; every separate phantasy contains the fulfilment of a wish, and improves an unsatisfactory reality. The impelling wishes vary according to sex, character and circumstances of the creator."[2] He also discovered that dreams are the conscious expression of unconscious phantasy. They have definite meaning as they are one of the normal manifestations of unconscious activity or wish. "The best known productions of phantasy are so called 'day-dreams',..., imagined satisfactions of ambitious, megalomanic, eratic wishes which flourish all the more exuberantly the more reality counsels modestry and restraint."[3] Freud has stressed on the role of phantasy and concluded that the source of creative impulse lies in some important unconscious phantasy. He has discovered that these phantasies are the driving factor for the emergence of art and creative writings. He believes that greater number of human beings create phantasies as long as they live. "As they grow up, people cease to play and appear to give up the pleasure they derived from play. But anyone who knows something of the mental life of human beings is aware that hardly anything is more difficult to them to give up a pleasure they have once tested. Really we never can relinquish anything, we only exchange something up, all we really do is adopt a substitute. So when human being grows up and ceases to play he only gives up the connection with real objects; instead of playing

1. Hendwick, Ives : Facts and theories of psycho-analysis, Alfred, A. Knoff, New York, 1958, p. 3.
2. Duhany, Don, E. (Ed.) : Contributions to modern psychology, Essay entitled, the relation of the poet to day dreaming by Sigmud Freud, Oxford Press, New York, p. 180.
3. Freud, S. : The Complete Introductory Lectures on Psychoanalysis, George Allen and Unwin, London, 1971, p. 372.

he then begins to create fantasy. He builds castles in the air and creates what are called day dreams."[4] The writer, according to Freud, does the same as the child at play; he creates a world of fantasy which he takes very seriously. That is why Freud calls imaginative writers as the day dreamers and their productions as day dreams. "His creations, works of art, were the imaginary gratifications of unconscious wishes, just as dreams are."[5]

Freud is primarily interested in the mechanism of human behaviour rather than the process of specialization. In his 'anatomy of human personality', he points out to the three processes of human mind viz. the unconscious, the preconscious, and the conscious. "Freud emphasises that these three terms—the unconscious, the pre-conscious, and the conscious—are the processes, not provinces or 'Systems' of the mind. The three realms, regions or provinces into which he decides the mental apparatus of the individual are Id, Ego and the Super Ego."[6]

"Id is that part of psychic functions which represents the instinctual drives in mental life and plays the role of stimulating or impelling the psychic apparatus to activity."[7] Ego is the surface part of the Id. "Its position determines its functions; it has to mediate between inside and outside happenings. This means that it has to recognise and become familiar with the events and objects in the outer world. The ego is not only the liason officer between Id, Superego and outside world, it is also the officer in command of the operation to be carried out by motor activity."[8] "The ego is what each of us means when he speaks of "Self", when he refers to "I". It comprises those

4. Freud, S. : Delusion and Dream and Other Essays, Edited by Philip Rieff, Relcon Press, Boston, 1956, p. 124.
5. Jones, E. : The Life and Work of Sigmund Freud, Vol. 3., Basic Book Inc. New York, 1957, p 421.
6. Ceillin J.L. : Cultural Sociology, Macmillan, New York, and Gillin G.P. 1954, p 656.
7. Sills, D.L. (Ed.) : Encylopedia of the Social Sciences, Vol. 13, Macmillan, New York, 1968, p. 5.
8. Klein, and Others : Developments in Psycho-analysis, The Hograth Press, London, 1952, p. 5.

elements of personality responsible for perceiving, knowing, reasoning, feeling, choosing, and also doing."[9] "The super ego represents the incorporation of parental attitudes which are determined by the existing cultural standards."[10]

Id is the oldest of these mental provinces. It contains everything that is inherited, that is present at birth and that is fixed in the constitution. Id obeys the pleasure principle. Its mental processes, subject to no laws of logic, are regarded as primary proces and are unconscious. The function of ego consists of interposing between Id demands and satisfying actions, intellectual activity aimed at calculating the consequences of any proposed behaviour. The ego must decide whether the satisfaction may be carried out or postponed or whether the demand of the instinct be altogether suppressed. If the main aim of the Id pleasure the main aim of the ego is safety.[11] The ego, as Freud observes, sometime plays the trick of identifying with the desire or Id to create a condition in which the Id can escape the ensure of the outer environment and the super ego. In the genesis of super ego the principle of child training prevailing in the society plays a significant role. According to Ann Freus, "Here it is not for the intervention of the ego or those of external forces which the ego represents, every instinct would have only one fate that of gratification."[12]

Community too, according to Freud, develops super ego and the super ego of any given epoch of civilization originates in the same way as that of of an individual. Freud also has thought about religion and explained it. "He calls attention to the close connection between the neurosis and religion in which he demonstrates———the remarkable resemblance between the psychic mechanism of obsession and those of religious ceremonials, both in their origin and development."[13]

9. Ives, Hendric : Op. cit., p. 147.
10 Smith, L and Strauss : Social psychology, Hoth, Rineheart and New York, 1956, p. 498
11. Kine, P. : Fact and Fantasy in Freudian Theory, Methuen Co. Ltd., London, 1972, p. 126.
12 Freud, A. : The Ego and The Mechanism of Defence, The Hograth Press and The Institute of Psycho analysis, London, 1954. p 47.
13. Britt, A.A. : Freud's Contribution to Psychiatry, Norton and Co., London, 1941, p. 198.

"The basic under current of all social actions and organisation", according to Freud, "is the sex impulse."[14] The sex instinct guides all our activities. According to Britt, "Freud forced us to talk objectively about sex and sexual motives. If you look up to the discussions of human behaviour written in the last century, you will be impressed by the complete omission of any material relating to sex. It is as if there had been a conspiracy among the authors to pretend that although men and women ate and slept and drank and carried on digestive activities, they were devoid of sex acts and feelings. But as a result of Freud's life long studies, people who are sincerely interested in human behaviour—psychologists, Sociologists, Social Workers, Clergymen, Lawyers, Physicians, Psychiatrists—have come more and more to realise that the interpretations of human behaviour depend to a great extent upon in understanding of sexual life of man and woman."[15] The term sexual, according to Freud, does not always mean sexual intercourse with opposite sex for the sake of pleasure or reproduction. It also includes a number of other acts e.g. Kissing, masturbation etc which are undoubtedly sexual but not directed towards reproduction. The definition of term sexual, therefore, seems to be difficult. We can, however, accept the popular view about the term which says, "sexual is something which combines references to the differences between the sexes, to pleasurable excitement and gratification, to the reproductive function and to the idea of impropriety and necessity for concealment."[16]

The human beings. according to Freud, are never free throughout their lives from sexual impulses. The Freudian theory also admits the existence of motive at the base of human behaviour and claims that the motives are of biological orgin. All motives are not equally conscious. Some of them are perfectly conscious and many others are perfectly uncons-

14. Sheriff, M and Sheriff, C.W. : An Outline of Social Psychology, Harper, New York, 1956, p. 340.
15. Britt, A.A. : Social Psychology of Modern Life, Holt, Rinehart, New York, p. 109.
16. Freud, S. : Introductory Lectures on Psycho-analysis, George Allen and Unwin, London, 1952, (9th impression), p. 256.

cious but the significant among them are either entirely or partly unconscious. Human personality is made out of conflicting motives. Every individual, according to Freud, is conscious about his, 'aim' which he persues though the sources of the urge are not always conscious. Moreover, he tries to achieve secondary aims in order to reach his conscious goal. An aim has an object. A simple example is the urge of hunger, the goal of which is to be satisfied and the object of which is food.[17]

Freud attempted to study the complexities of human personality and found a relationship between the mental structure and the social experiences. "Individual development seems to us a product of interplay of two trends, the striving for happiness, generally called egoistic and the impulse towards marging with pathers in the community, which we call altruistic."[18] Our primitive urges are suppressed and disciplined by the human culture which acts as an agency. "It is the principal thesis of Freud that society suppresses human impulses, that the social order is built on instinctual repression."[19] The basic sources of energy, as a consequence of such repression, are channelised through cultural forms. Freud says, "However proud we may be of our cultural achievement it is by no means easy to satisfy the requirements of this civilisation and to feel comfortable in its midst, because the restriction of the instinct which it involves lays a heavy psychological burden on our shoulders."[20]

Freud has divided the early years of life of an individual into three phases in terms of the dominance of a particular sensitive zone viz. oral, anal and genital or phallic and presented a theory of psycho-sexual development of personality. "The first of these pregenital phases is known to us as

17. Alexander, F. and Ross, H. : Dynamic Psychiatry (Essay entitled—History of Metapsychological concepts by E. Weiss), Univ. of Chicago, 1952, pp. 44-46.
18 Freud, S. : Civilization and Its discontent, Hograth Press, London, 1956, p. 134.
19. Asch, S.E. : Social Psychology, Prentice Hall, New York, 1922, (7th printing), p. 17.
20. Freud, S. : A New Series of Introductory Lectures on Psychoanalysis, Norton, London, 1933, p. 151.

the oral one because, in confirmity with the way in which an infant in arms is nourished, the erotogenic zones of the mouth dominates what may be called the sexual activity of that period of life. At a second level the sadistic and anal impulses come to the fore, undoubtedly in connection with the appearance of the teath, the strengthening of the muscular apparatus and the control of the sphincter functions."[21] "The third general stage is called Oedipal or phalic, because the child's sexual urges—now become intensified and directed toward the parent of the opposite sex—the mother is the object of the boy's first hetro-sexual interest—Freud postulated that the sight of the male genitals arouses 'Penis envy' in the girls, and that is instrumental in breaking the girl and—the girl is said to turn towards the father. However, sometimes after lengthy conflict and vacillation, the girl develops her own kind of Oedipus complex—the electra complex—The boy is in competition with his father for the mother, but can not win. Although he can not actually consummate his urges, he feels guilty and expects retaliation to be directed toward the organ from which he receives pleasure. The fear of castration—mutilation—develops, in varying intensity, even if a threat of physical punishment was never uttered. Fear of castration brings about ambivalance towards the father. The boy tries to please him by identification with his non-sexual areas of behaviour and tends also to idealise him."[22]

According to Krech and Crutch Field, "Emphasis of the Freudian in primarily upon the genetic problem with the implication that behaviour can not adequately be explained in terms of the properties of the immediate psychological situation but must be referred back to the past history of the person. Thus to understand why a certain individual is ready to lead a revolt against a political authority, an orrhodox Freudian might invoke the oedipus complex in his historical motivational analysis of this individual's social behaviour—characterising the oedipus stage is the need to kill the father

21. Freud, S. : The Complete Introductory Lectures on Psycho-analysis, Op. cit , p. 562.
22. Smith, L. and Strauss : Op. cit., p. 555-556.

and possess the mother. This need is, of course, repressed but the hostility against the father may manifest itself in the development of a general aggression against the political head of the state."[23]

An outline of the Freudian theory, discussed above, may help the readers to appreciate the prevalence of the same in the Urdu novels. Understanding of the Freudian theory, even in a precise form, facilitate the task of content analysis. The urdu novelists belonging to the Freudian school have almost declared their faith in the concept of 'Pan sexualism' and applied the same in their novels. For the purpose of content analysis and to trace the impact of Freudian theory, some major novels written by prominent urdu novelists viz. Wadda by Mahinder Nath, Toofan Aur Sahil by Gulshan Nanda, Aurat, Daulat Aur Shohart by Dat Bharti, Anke Banke by Hans Raj Rahbar, and Chai-Ke-Baagh by Qurratul Ain Haider have been taken into consideration.

Following is the content analysis of the novels mentioned above :

CONTENT ANALYSIS OF SOME NOVELS BEARING FREUDIAN INFLUENCES

1. '*Waada*' *by Mahindar Nath*

Character

Usha.

How Identified

A girl belonging to a lower middle class family of urban society. She is very much idealist in temperament and consequently nonflexible in character. By profession she is a stage artist in a dramatic company and falls in love with Dilip who is an actor in the drama as well as an author.

23. Krech, D. and Crutchfield, R.S. : The Theory and Problems of Social Psychology, McGraw-Hill, New York, 1948, p. 35.

Treatment in the Novel

Usha has been treated as the heroine of the novel. Her idealistic temperament created a sense of aversion for such persons without moded ideas and narrow outlook. She, like majority of the young girls, preferred to marry a man of standard as well as suited to her liking. She developed romantic attachment with Dilip, a coworker in her profession and an author, inspite of the fact that the later was a married man, because of his strong personality and radical ideas. Unfortunately, Dilip's wife died in the meantime and her death made Usha completely purturbed. She held herself as responsible for the death of Dilip's wife. As a result she decided not to marry Dilip and to spend her life in serving her parents, sisters and brothers.

Dominant Traits in the Character consistent with Freudian Idea

Firstly, the presence of idealism in the character of Usha reminds the reader about the strong super ego which she possessed. Secondly, her will power as well as the sense of determination was quite strong.

Thirdly, the process of the sublimation of sex is obviously marked in her character.

Fourthly, the aggressive tendency is also marked in her character. This is known by her desire to go against the traditional pattern of life.

Lastly, we mark the development of a complex or more specifically, the guilt complex in Usha.

The presence of complex and their impact on human behaviour or personality is a typical contribution of Freudian theory.

Some Statement consistent with Freudian Ideology contained in the Novel

1. 'Usha learned from her very childhood to talk fearlessly and to criticise things which were not correct to insist on any thing that her mind or heart accepted, and also not to surrender her individuality to other'.

2. 'She wanted to marry such an individual who could feed her mentally as well as physically. In other words she wanted both mental and physical satisfaction from her husband. Moreover she desired that her husband should be such a man who could command regard as well as the respect of others and also could justify her selection as really appreciable.'

3. 'Her unusual behaviour pattern was the result of the displacement of her sexual urge. How long the sexual instinct could be suppressed?

4. 'A woman can sacrifice anything for love she can do anything; she can fight with her relatives and neglect the entire world society.'

5. 'Dilp took Usha into his arms and embraced her, also kissed her.'

6. 'One who does not love a beautiful woman he is not entitled to be called as a man.'

7. 'But I love pleasure and the satisfaction of my desires. When I saw you, I tried to captivate you but I knew that you are lost in the arms of another woman.'

8. 'Dilip take this glass and kiss it before you return it to me...Dilip I have sold my love and purchased wine . . . I have sold my chastity and purchased this house. You did not see me during my young days. If you had seen me at that time probably you might not have been able to control yourself.'

9. 'Dilip in the name of God I say that I never loved you, I never loved any body but I wanted every man I came in contact with and that is why I am still alive.'

10. 'Radha knows the art of concealing her pains. Poverty has taught her many things. She knows the art of laughing in the midst of sorrow.'

11. 'I don't know the reason for my hatred to Usha. She is not a suitable girl for you. She is not beautiful. You should marry a beautiful girl with charming dispositions.'

Character

Dilip

How Identified

An author and at the same time a stage artist. He used to act in dramas.

Treatment in the Novel

Dilip is the hero of the novel. He belongs to a lower middle class family of Bombay and lives in one of the many slums of the city. He is married to Radha, a woman with no education and also without any sophistication. On the whole Dilip is a poor man with a meagre income and leads a life devoid of any encouragement and romanticism.

In other words he is deprived of the life which he has aspired and this deprivation leads him to fall in love with Usha, a girl unlike his wife Radha. Usha, whom Dilip loves as soon as they meet each other in a drama rehearsal, is an educated girl with sophisticated behaviour. In fact, Usha resembles very much with the image of a beloved which Dilip cherishes in his mind for a long time. Usha, unlike Radha, is capable of appreciating the talents of Dilp and this gives him immense pleasure and a sense of satisfaction. Dilip feels no remorse rather a sense of delight when his wife Radha dies. This is very remarkable in his character and also quite consistent to the Freudian idea. The dichotomy of the conscious and unconscious mind is made clear by this trail of Dilip's mind.

Dominant Traits in the Character Consistent with Freudian Idea

Firstly, Dilip was guided more by the 'pleasure principle' than the 'reality principle'. He wanted the satisfaction of his desires.

Secondly, the craze for physical comforts and the selfish approach for getting these comforts makes it clear that Dilip was not only pleasure seeking but at the same time an ego centic individual. The defence of ego against Id, in his character was not effective.

Thirdly, we find an abundance of selfishness in his character.

Fourthly, he possessed an aggressive instinct but not sufficiently strong.

Fifthly, the repression of sex is quite obvious in his character and this makes him somewhat sadistic in temperament.

Sixthly, the character of Dilip makes clear the idea of interrelatedness and interdependence of the masculine and feminine existence.

Lastly, Dilip's character reminds us of the basic principle of sex psychology which says that in contrast with the female the male gives only a part of his self to the female.

Character

Meera

How Identified

A society girl and crazy for comforts and satisfaction of even instinctive, desires.

Treatment in the novel

The character of Meera represents the class of such women in the modern society whom we know as society girls. Meera as appears from the description of the author, had no fastidiousness about the chastity, virginity, virtue and vice etc. which have almost become outdated and at the same time unrealistic concepts in the modern materialistic society. She considered the instinctive pleasure above all other things and loved to live in the midst of plenty. She maintained a high standard of living and at the same time the acceleration of her life was also quite fast. She possessed a good physique and also quite apt in dancing. She was attracted towards Dilip and wanted him for sexual pleasure. But inspite of her perfect coquetry she failed to captivate Dilip. This created a sense of frustration and she developed a deep seated jealousy for Usha whom Dilip loved.

Dominant Traits in the Character consistent with Freudian Idea

Firstly, the author has pointed out the predominance of instinctive urges and particularly sex in Meera's character.

Secondly, the presence of aggressive instinct is quite obviously marked in her character.

Thirdly, we find an indication about the presence of a strong Narcissus complex in her character which is a significant discovery of Freud in the field of psycho-analysis.

Fourthly, we find the dominance of pleasure principle over the reality principle in this character.

Fifthly, the dominance of the pleasure principle also suggests the dominance of Id in her character.

Sixthly, she had a weak super-ego.

Lastly, we also notice her jealousy for Usha which according to Freud is commonly found in love.

Character

Radha

How Identified

Wife of Dilip, the hero of the novel. An orphan who learnt many realities of life in the midst of the adverse circumstances of life.

Treatment in the Novel

The character of Radha has been painted by the author as a helpless orphan girl who was deprived of the parental affection in her childhood and that very unfortunate incident had left its impression on the character and the behaviour of the poor girls. She was a pretty girl with humble demeanor and very limited span of desires. That humbleness was the rusult of her living in a very poor family during her childhood. On the whole Radha seems to be an ideal character which fits as the house wife in an Indian family with a very moderate income. Radha came in contact with Dilip while she was working as an extra in the cine industry. After their marriage she completely identified with her husband and was quite happy. But gradually the situation took an adverse turn and Dilip started spending most of his time with Usha. This made Radha extremely jealous and she also developed a sense of hatred for Dilip. This state of affairs naturally caused much strain and affected her health adversely. Ultimately she died of tuberculosis.

Dominant Traits in the Character consistent with Freudian Idea

Firstly, a deep sense of devotion and sacrifice is marked in the character of Radha. This is quite consistent with Freudian idea. According to Freud this is the outcome of the phenomenon of identification which the women often develop with their husbands after marriage.

Secondly, the jealousy is also found in her character which according to Freud is quite commonly found in the affairs of love.

Thirdly, the character of Radha is characterised with the existence of a strong super-ego.

Fourthly, the ego is stronger than the aggressive tendency in her character.

Lastly, a feeling of frustration is also clearly marked in her character which she had developed as a result of the loss of confidence in her husband.

2. *Toofan Aur Sahil by Gulshan Nanda*

Character

Anand

How Identified

Sales Manager of a commercial firm. He was a bachelor with handsome personality and belonged to a middle class family.

Treatment in the Novel

Leading character of the novel. He loved Sindhia, daughter of a rich man known as Roy Sahib, whom he met in connection with a business deal with Roy Sahib. But subsequently he was introduced to Bela, the younger sister of Sindhia, and developed an infatuaticn for her. The relationship between them culminated into sexual union and as a result Bela forced Anand to marry her. The marital life of Bela and Anand, however, proved a failure. In course of time the infatulation of Anand for Bela subsided and he did not feel himself attracted to Bela. On the other hand his love for Sindhia made him very much frustrated and he held Beta as responsible for the tragedy in his life.

Dominant Traits in the Character consistent with Freudian Idea

Firstly, the urge for sexual pleasure is quite clearly marked in the character of Anand. He used to love a girl but developed infatuation for her younger sister. The temptation of sex was definitely stronger than his devotion to the girl he loved.

Secondly, we find that Anand was guided more by Id impulses than any other factor.

Thirdly, the conflict between the unconscious impulse and the super-ego led to the growth of contradictory trends in his character.

Finally, we find that in his marital life Anand was unsuccessful. He was not happy with his wife. This is quite consistent with the idea that sex minus emotion or love is often quite short lived and in the absence of love infatuation dies within a short perion.

Some Statement consistent with Freudian Ideology contained in the Novel

1. 'Bela is like fire but at the same time quite thrilling. She is undoubtedly more beautiful than Sindhia. Her youth is full of attractions. Her every action creates turmoil in my heart and invigorates me. I am quite young and it is not a sin on my part to drag her and hold her in an embrace'.

2. 'Though I am a woman, I am fighting against the odds and you being a male feeling disappointed. Remember that

true love demands sacrifice. The real life is that which one lives for others and not for his own self.'

3. 'I am more beautiful than my elder sister. If she can play with the heart of Anand than why not my eyes can lit the fire of love in his heart.'

4. 'I possess that type of beauty which can make you people start dancing'.

5. In no way I am inferior to Sindhia. My education, family brckground, physical charm are not inferior to her. What more you need to make true love with me? Moreover, in order to satisfy you I have given every thing of mine without much resistence.'

6. 'Please hold me in your arms as you hold my elder sister . . . she kissed his lips.'

7. 'She rubbed her face on Anand's chest and said in a whispering tone—what you have done to me Anand ? I am standing on the bank of the river but you do not allow me to quench my thirst.

Character

Sindhia.

How Identified

A beautiful young girl of rich family. Though she was born in a poor home she was brought up in the midst of plenty. She was sophisticated but at the same time very much sympathetic and kind hearted to those who deserved that.

Treatment in the Novel

Heroine of the novel. She loved Anand and wanted to marry him but she decided otherwise when she came to learn about the sexual union of Anand with Bela, her younger sister. She rather forced Anand to marry Bela and diverted her energy towards the welfare of the poor and needy people. She started a small scale industry with an intention to provide livelihood to some poor people. She was a girl with strong will power and determination. She was quite magnanimous in her dealings with Anand and Bela. Whenever the situation demanded she ungrudgingly rendered her serviees. She ultimately lost her life while attempting to save the lives of the working in her factory from a cyclonic stron which devasted their colony.

Dominant Traits in the Character consistent with Freudian Idea

Firstly, we find the sublimation of sex due to non-fulfilment or frustration and the diversion of the energy towards humanitarian activities.

Secondly, the author has also pointed out the presence of a strong super-ego in Sindhia and that made her an idealist.

Thirdly, the tendency more correctly the readiness for sacrifice of self interest is marked in her character. Freud claims that the act of self sacrifice is needed for the fulfilment of love.

Lastly, the eros appears to be stronger than the aggressive tendency in the character of Sindhia.

Character

Bela.

How Identified

A student of B.A. (final) class of Delhi University. Belonged to a rich family. She was quite modern in her outlook and believed in full freedom of choice. She was smart, beautiful and a fashionable young lady.

Treatment in the Novel

Bela is an important character of the novel. She has been treated as the younger sister of Sindhia, the heroine of the story. Bela was extremely beautiful and smart. Moreover, she was very much conscious of her physical charm and attractiveness. That made her a bit arrogant in her behaviour. She had fallen in love with Anand in spite of her knowledge that the later was in love with her elder sister. She practically seduced Anand to establish sexual relationship with her. She was extremely selfish aud jealous. For the sake of physical comfort and fulfilment of desires she did not hesitate even to kill her brother in law and made an attempt on the life of her mother-in-law. She was not against the artificiality in life and considered sex as more important in the relationship between man and woman than love. She preferred to go for an abortion after her marriage than loosing her physical charm by giving birth to a child. But the death of her sister, Sindhia was quite shocking to her and that could bring a total transformation in her mind. She changed herself and started a new life.

Dominant Traits in the Character consistent with Freudian Idea

In the character of Bela the following trails consistent with Freudian theory are remarked :

1. Strong urge for sex.
2. Non-identification with her husband.
3. Existence of aggressive tendency.
4. The sense of jealously for her elder sister whom she considered as her rival in love.
5. Predominance of Id and at the same time a weak super-ego.
6. The craze for physical comforts and the selfish approach for getting those comforts reminds us that Bela was not only a pleasure seeking but also an ego centric girl.
7. The tendency for exibitionism is marked in her character which is at the same time an indication of the Nacissus complex in Bela.
8. Bela's character also introduced the reader to the Freudian concept of the regressian of behaviour pattern which is marked by a transformation of rhe normal behaviour pattern of an individual.

3. '*Aurat, Daulat Aur Shorat*' *by Dut Bharti*

Character

Sheo Datt

How Identified

Belonged to a middle class family. He started his career as a dramatist but later on he switched over to Films industry and directed many films quite successfully. That brought him reputation, fame and wealth. He married a beautiful girl names Rita but his conjugal life was disturbed. Inspite of material happiness and prosperity he was disgrunted and frustrated.

Treatment in the Novel

Sheo Datt appears as the central character in the story. The author has portrayed the inner life of Sheo Datt and analysed the various innate forces which played dominant roles in his personality.

Sheo Datt was very much sensitive and emotional. He loved Rita and married her but he could not get emotional satisfaction and that became a cause for conjugal disharmony. His love for Rita was based on her physical attraction and outer appearance. In other words sex was the primary consideration for his attraction towards Rita. The frustration in marital life made him a sadist and he started deriving pleasure out of pain. Inspite of his knowledge regarding the adulterous acts of his wife Rita, he did not break with her but became addicted to wine. That ultimately cut his life short and he died at an early age.

Dominnnt Traits in the Character consistent with Freudian Idea

1. The dominence of ego in his personality is clearly marked. He believed in material prosperity and physical

comforts. In order to achieve his goal he was motivated to earn lot of money in film industry.

2. The author has pointed out that the sexual instinct guided the behaviour of Sheo Datt who selected his life partner not because of emotional attachment, rather he gave more emphasis on the physical charm and beauty.

3. We also find that his unhappy marital life made him extremely frustrated and he developed sadistic tendencies. Due to that development he derived pleasure in pain.

4. We also mark the existence of suicide complex in Sheo Datt. This complex resulted due to the diversion of his aggressive tendencies towards in own self or ego.

Some Statement consistent with freudian Iedology contained in the Novel

"During this period of 11 years you have been embracing and maintaining sexual relationship with him . . . whenever you embraced me you thought of him. Whenever you kissed me his image appeared in your mind. Even at the time of sexual intercourse with me you always thought of him."

" . . . is it not true that my life has been confined to wine? Should I destroy my position, fame and wealth as you have not yet forgotton your lover? You have broken the sanctity of the marital life."

"Previously he could stay without women for a maximum period of five days but now the limit has been lowered to the period of only three days."

Character

Rita

How Identified

Heroine of the novel. Belongs to an upper middle class family. An ultramodern educated girl. She had an extreme craze for physical comforts. Sexually she was delinquent and established sexual relation with her tenant at an early age. She married Sheo Datt because of his promising career but even after marriage she indulged in extra marital sexual relationship with Mahinder, one of the friends of her husband Sheo Datt.

Treatment in the Novel

She is the heroine of the novel. Through her character the author has attempted to describe the significance of sex instinct in determining the direction of human behaviour. Rita was very much guided by her sex-instinct. When she became young she developed sexual relation with her tenant. But when he wanted to marry her Rita refused because he was a poor man. She believed in physical comforts as well as pleasure of life and so she decided to marry Sheo Datt who had a promising career. But even after marriage she continued her Illicit sexual relationship with Mahinder. She loved sexual pleasure so much that she did not hesitate to enjoy it even after the death of her husband and her son.

She had an extreme sense of self-preservation. She wanted to keep her husband totally in her clutches and did not tolerate even the friends and relatives of her husband. As a result all the relatives and friends left Sheo Datt alone. She developed a sense of jealousy against them and always tried to have the entire attention of her husband. This selfish attitude and dominance of sexual instincts led her to suffer from psychological complex which created a contradiction in her personality. The lust for comfortable life and worldly pleasure were the basic trails of her personality. As a result she could neither be a devoted wife nor a loving mother.

Dominant Traits in the Character consistent with Freudian Idea

1. The pre-dominance of sexual urge is clearly marked in the character of Rita.

2. We also find an extreme sense of jealousy in Rita who did not tolerate the presence of any relative and friend of her husband.

3. The lust for pleasure and comfortable life is also distinct in her character.

4. The author has also depicted the selfish attitude of Rita which was due to the sense of self-preservation.

5. Aggressiveness is also reflected in her personality as she always tried to dominate over her husband.

6. Non-identification with her husband is also quite obvious.

7. In the character of Rita we mark a peculiar trait that her sexual urge and the emotional attachment could not meet at the same point. She maintained her illicit connections with Mahinder even after marriage but at the same time she loved her husband. This makes us sure about the existence of the opposite trends within her personality.

8. An overall analysis of Rita's character reveals that she was motivated more by unconscious desires of Id according to Freudian terminology and at the same time she was ego centric. Her pleasure seeking nature is a sufficient indication of the dominant Id in her personality. Her super-ego was weak.

Some Statement consistent with freudian Ideology in the Novel

"I feel that every art is the reflection of life or nature of the artist. That's why it is said that an artist is understood by this artistic works."

" . . . and you have not loved him rather you have married him only due to your sexual urge."

"Every artist has a source of inspiration . . . if a woman is a source of inspiration for a man then why not a man can be a source of inspiration for a woman."

"If an artist, who is struggling with the unusual circumstances, gets a woman who encourages him after he comes back to his residence he will not feel frustrated in his life."

" . . . I am the only daughter of my father . . . I want to marry a boy of my own choice. I never like a clerk whose life is just like silent lake without any ripple and who moves within a specific circle."

"If I am prevented I will run away with you from this house taking the valuable ornament as well as cash . . . and I will have you at any cost."

"I am fully confident that one day you will become a big man and you will achieve fame as well as wealth. Because of this confidence in you I can marry you."

"Rita can exploit any one for her self interest and she never cares to think of her behaviour with the person afterwards."

Character

Shashi

How Identified

Belonged to a lower middle class family. She was a neighbour of Sheo Datt. She was very much gentle and a submissive girl. She used to speak less but always tried to assist Sheo Datt's sister-in-demostic works. Due to her frequent visit to Sheo Datt's home she developed attachment with all the family members of Sheo Datt and had developed the feeling of love for him.

Treatment in the Novel

She is one of the important characters of the novel. Though her appearance in the story is for a short period the impact of her character is quite enduring. She had fallen in love with Sheo Datt but could not express or disclose her love to him. Her love was full of sacrifice when she was married to some body else she committed suicide on the very first night of her marriage.

Dominant Traits in the Character consistent with Freudian Idea

1. The concept of platonic love is quite clearly marked in the character of Shashi.

2. In her character we find that she was sympathetic to Sheo Datt and this sympathy created the falling of love in her mind for Sheo Datt. This is quite consistent with Freudian idea.

3. Presence of an extreme sense of sacrifice and dedication in the character of Shashi has been pointed out by the author.

4. A complete identification of Sashi with Sheo Datt is also marked and that ultimately led her to commit suicide. According to the Freudian concept suicide is the end result of the conflict between ego and aggressive instinct.

5. Her super-ego was well developed.

4. *'Aanke-Banke' by Hans Raj Rahbar.*

Character

Rajendar Pal.

How Identified

A journalist working in a newspaper owned by a capitalist. Belongs to a middle class family. Progressive in his ideas.

Treatement in the Novel

Hero of the novel. He was an idealist and planned his own way of life by breaking old traditions and conventions. He started his career as a journalist with a view to lead an independent life. He married a divorced woman—Kalpana, whom he loved because of her strong personality and progressive ideas. Though he married Kalpana with an agreement that there could be no interference in the private affairs of each other but basically he wanted to dominant over her. As a result conflict arose among them and that created strain in their conjugal life. At the request of his wife he joined a theatre company started by her but he became very much frustrated by the behaviour of his wife and ultimately be left both his wife and the theatre company. He came back to his parents' house and started his life afresh after giving up his ideal concept of life and decided to live in accordance with the traditional customs and conventions of the society.

Dominant Traits in the Charaeter consistent with Freudian Idea

1. The leaning towards idealism in the character of Rajendra Pal is an indication of a strong super-ego in him.

2. Due to his strong will power he planned his own way of life and rejected all traditional and customary ways of loving.

3. The author has pointed out the psychological complex which has been termed by Freud as 'Oedipus complex' in the character of Rajendar Pal.

4. The Freudian concept of regression of beliour is also marked in this character.

5. Lastly, the author has suggested the existence of a strong sexual urge in the character of Rajendra Pal and that made him to decide to marry Kalpana, a girl with much sexual appeal.

Some Statement consistent with Freudian Ideology contained in the Novel

"....I have established marital relationship with Kalpana according to my own wish. I was very much happy that I could break all the customs and traditions—but now I have realised that the basis of our relation was sexual desire and not love."

"....It means that the basis of marriage was the sexual hunger for a woman and not simply love."

"Your revolt was merely a temporary phase and its basis was sexual desire."

"Without woman life is dull and unpleasant. You have acted wisely to marry. Now at least you have a woman."

"And I have come to this conclusion on the basis of my experience that a woman is a great reality in this world and she is the soul of all literature and philosophy."

"Man is also eager to get appreciation from a woman."

Charater

Kalpana

How Identified

Belonged to a middle class family. She was a good dancer and a theatre artist. She was a lady with strong will power and determination. She always opposed *traditional* way of life and planned her own way of living. She did not allow even her husband to interfere in her private affairs.

Treatment in the Novel

Heroine of the novel. She was the wife of Rajendar Pal. It was her second marriage. Her first marriage did not continue for a long time because her first husband was very much orthodox. She wanted to lead her life with full freedom and liberty and she did not tolerate any interference in her private life.

She had an extreme sense of exhibitionism. As she was a good dancer and a stage artist, she wanted to display her talent on the stage in order to get recognition and appreciation from the public. In order to satisfy this urge she started her own theatre, company.

The character of Kalpana emerges as a great challenge to the traditional Indian Society which do not permit woman to stand at par with males in various spheres of life.

Another important feature of Kalpana's character was that she had no feeling of sacrifice. She remained with her husband (Pal) till both of them did not interfered in the affairs of each other but when the agreement of non-interference failed she left him without much hesitation.

Dominant traits in the Character consistant with Freudian Idea

1. The character of Kalpana reflected the dominance of super-ego.

2. But at the same time she was egoistic and due to this opposing characteristic her personality lacked consistency. Whatever she decided to do she did without any consideration for other's sentiment.

3. She was guided by her innate instincts.

4. She had an extreme sense of exhibitionism.

5. She believed in freedom and opposed all restraints and restrictions.

6. She had no feeling of sacrifice for others and was motivated chiefly by 'Pleasure Principle'.

Some Statement Consistent with Freudian Ideology contained in the Novel

"You don't believe in any boundage. I also do not believe in it because we want free life and also to lead a comfortable life.

"It means that you always want your wishes and desires to be imposed on your wife like other males. Has a woman got no existence of her own? Has she got no right to lead her free life in a way to fullfil her wishes and desires."

"I know very well that I have no prestige in this house and I am treated like a prostitute. If you want to stay here you can do so but I cannot stay here for a moment".

"When a woman doesnot get love nothing in the world can give her pleasure."

Character

Rekha

How Identified

An ultramodern woman of middle class family. Addicted to wine and accustomed with having many boy friends. Working in a theatre company. Vulgar and cheap in her performance.

Treatment in the Novel

She is an important character in the story of this novel. The novelist has pointed out the dominance of sexual instincts in her character and also her tendency to break the traditional concept of sexual ethics and she was leading a life free from all restraints. She left her husband and joined a theatre company in order to lead a free life. She was of the view that a woman had complete right to establish sex relations with any body she wanted even after marriage.

Dominant Traits in the Character consistent with Freudian Idea

1. The character of Rekha reflects a strong sense of sex which made her to turn into a pleasure seeking woman.

2. Another important characteristic of her personality is her aggressiveness. She had broken all the concept of sexual ethics and led a free life.

Some Statement consistent with Freudian Ideology contained in the Novel

"A woman is free to love anybody...even after marriage."

". . . . the relation of man and woman is natural but marriage is a social restrain. The natural love turns into an artificial life when one is married . . . . and gradually the relationship comes at the verge of decay."

". . . . if a man can not obey a woman then why a woman will obey a man ?

"Man is very much eager to get appreciation from his friends and relatives. For this he does not sleep in the night and labours hard. Admiration is a great charm which inspires a writer to produce creative literature without any care for his hunger and comfort."

"There has always been differences between principles and practices. One who understands this difference becomes successful in his life."

Character

Lala Gobardhan

How Identified

A capitalist. Owner of a daily news paper named, 'Sandesh' and also an insurance company. A man with political inclination but at the same time selfish and opportunist. He had lust for wealth.

Treatment in the Novel

One of the leading characters in the novel. Though he was born and brought up in a poor family but due to his selfishness and opportunistic ideas he could manage to make black money.

He believed that there had been always difference between principles and practices and those who could know this differeace he could lead a successful life. He satisfied his ego with the wealth of which he thought to be the only factor through which pleasure could be achieved.

Dominant Traits in the Character consistent with Freudian Idea

1. The presence of an extreme sense of selfishness as well as opportunism in the character of Gobardhan was due to his weak super-ego.
2. His lust for wealth at the same time was the indication of the predominance of the ego in his personality.
3. He also believed in what Freud has termed as 'Pleasure Principle'.

5. *'Chai-Ki-Baagh' by Qurratul Ain-Haider*

Character

Raahat

How Identified

A pleasure seeking ultra-modern girl. Though she was born in a middle class Muslim family she always identified herself as the member of a rich family. Once she accepted the job of an Asst. Information Officer in war publicity department.

Treatment in the Novel

One of the important characters of the novel. The author has analysed the various characteristics of her personality in order to explain her inner self. Raahat was very much materialistic and wanted to enjoy all the luxeries of life. Though she was born and brought up in a middle class family but the hardship caused by the poor economic condition and lust for pleasure led her to escape from the realities of life and take recourse to 'day dreaming'. She wanted to forget her unpleasant experiences of life and with that intention she endeavoured to change her identity by changing her name.

Raahat married twice; first time at Calcutta and second time at Bombay. But she did not continue her relations with either of her husbands for a long time. Later on she went to East Pakistan and could lead a romantic life by indulging herself in the love making with few persons in the upper strata of the society. She was a girl motivated chiefly by pleasure principle and with much of sex appeal. In other words she preferred a happy-go-lucky way of living and evaded the realities and responsibilities of life.

Dominant Traits in the Character consistent with Freudian Idea

Firstly, we find an extreme craze for pleasure in the character of Raahat. She wanted to enjoy the luxuries of life and comfort more than anything else.

2. Secondly, a sense of exhibitionism is clearly marked in her character and she was pround of her physical charm as well as sex appeal.

3. Thirdly, we mark the strong sexual urge in her character.

4. Fourthly, the exhibitionism found in her character was due to the presence of a strong narcisus complex in her personality.

Fifthly, the day dreaming of Raahat was mainly due to the existence of a sense of escapism in her character.

Lastly, she suffered from inferiority complex.

Some Statements consistent with Freudian Ideology contained in the Novel

1. "All the problems relating to human body depend upon its approach. Doctors have clinical approach while poets, sculptors and painters believe in aesthetic or sexual approach which may be either healthy or neurotic . . . . ."

2. "Raahat called me in her bathroom. That reflected her deep sense of exhibitionism. She had an awareness about her beauty as well as her body."

3. ". . . . I discovered that a girl who always lives in day dreams, thinks herself as Marelin Munro, who is talking with her lovers, directors and producers of international repute and lying in the golden bath tub in Holly Wood."

4. ". . . it was a great tragedy for her that inspitc of her extra ordinary beauty, intelligence, artistic ability and other qualities she could not get anything. Because of that she developed a feeling of inferiority complex and frustration."

5. "I know that Raahat feels herself very much insecured and wants to attach herself to one of those people with a strong footing in life."

Character

Farhat

How Identified

Sister of Raahat. She had the same qalities like her sister.

Treatment in the Novel

The main features of Farhat's character were much similar to her elder sister—Raahat. Though she was married to an eminent film actor of Bombay, she continued her sexual relationship with a number of rich persons. Entire activities of Farhat were guided by the lust for pleasure of life. She created trouble in the conjugal life of many families. She was selfish, unethical and at the same time irresponsible in her actions.

Dominant Traits in the Character consistent with Freudian Idea

Firstly, Farhat, like her elder sister Raahat, was chiefly guided by the Id and that made her pleasure seeking.

Secondly, the unethical trends in her character was an indication of the feable super-ego which she possessed.

Thirdly, the selfishness in her character was the symptom of her egocentric tendency.

Lastly, the lack of rationality and predominance of instinctive tendencies caused a strong urge for sexual pleasure in her mind.

Charactor

Sanober

How Identified

Her real name was Sadiqua. Daughter of an important person of Assam. Her mother was an English lady. Her first marriage was solmanised with major Shamshad but later on she took divorce and was married to one of Shamshad's friend Mr. Qasim. But her second married life was also not happy and again she was separated from Qasim to marry Wajid.

Treatment in the Novel

The psychological complex and frustration in married life of Sanober have been explained by the author. Her first marriage was arranged by her father Dr. Zafar Ali with Major Shamshad who loved his wife deeply and also admired her. As a token of his love he gave a new name, Sanoner, to his wife, But soon after the marriage Major Shamshad went to Cairo in connection with his job and in his absence Sanober came in contact with one of his friends Qasim and indulged in sexual intercourse with him. Later on she divorced her husband and married Quasim. But the second marriage did not continue and again she married Wajid for the third time after being separated from Quaism. The author has pointed out the presence of selfishness in the character of Sanober. She was more concerned about her own self and failed to develop a sense of devotion to any of her three husbands. Consequently, her life became a failure and she ended up in the deep sense of frustration as well as despair.

Dominant Traits in the Character consistent with Freudian Idea

1. The author has pointed out that Sanober was mainly an ego eentric woman.
2. The super-ego was not properly developed.
3. Sex played a dominant role in determining the courses of her life.
4. She also possessed the electra complex.
5. Presence of aggressive tendency was marked in her character. That was quite normal for a woman with a strong ego like Sanober.

Some Statements consistent with Freudian Ideology contained in the Novel

"He says that Farhat is just like all other women for him. She entered in his life as a complete woman few years ago and now she has again come in his life and as such he can not leave her."

Conclusion

(I)

Literature and sociology are two distinct disciplines with different premises as well as methods, but attempts have been made to explore common ground and as a result interesting works in the area have been produced by sociologists. The writer is neither solitary nor autonomous. He is bound by his time, and lives within its horizons and draws the potential for thought and vision. He is also bound by a body of practices, conventions, and percepts, bound by the orders and structures with which he shapes and designs his material, and by much more practical conventions of his profession and his craft, such as those which tell him what a novel, a poem, or play is, as exchangrable object. Thus, literature is the storehouse of all the motive content handed over to society by the collective mind of people for its subsistence and nourishment. We may, therefore, dream a people's literature to be an index of their social life or culture. As is the social condition and status of a people, so shall be their literature. A writer's obligation to society is to give expression to his own personality—a combination of experience, ideas, environmental influences, emotions and sensibilities. No man can escape the influence of social forces while trying to expose his personality. In the words of Aldous Huxley, "life affects literature by first affecting the men and women who produce that literature; and these men and women will react to the pressures and stimuli of the environment in different ways, according to their varous temperaments and constitutions."[1] If we survey the treasure of urdu novels published in India during 1947 to 1967, we can very well conclude that urdu novelists have successfully projected the vision of the changing Indian society—its operative forces, prevailing system of social organization, the class structure, the economic system, the political organization, the dominant ideas etc. They transmit images of behaviour, emotions and attitudes, social and personal standards in the heterogenous rapidly changing democratic Indian society.

The birth of novel in urdu can be taken no further back than the age of Nazir Ahmad and Ratan Nath Sarshar in the late 19th and early 20th century. The early 20th century marked the period when the development of modern social outlook started as a result of our contact with the people of the West, especially the literary values of the Romantics which percolated to the educated middle class people in India. Hence the first pre-occupation of the early novelists was with love, beauty, women, social reform and humanism. Since its birth, the urdu novel has come a long way. The survey of the thematic variety may lead to this conclusion that it has developed in several directions, for instance, in the field of social realism and cultural depiction, of psychological analysis, of delineation of characters, of politics and sex, and of symbolic and allegorical representation of the contemporary realities. The modern urdu novel is indebted to Krishan Chandar, Khaja Ahmad Abbas, Rajendra Singh Bedi, Balwant Singh, Ali Abbas Hussaini, Saleha Abid Hussain, Qarrutal Ain Haider, Qazi Abdus Sattar, Ismat Chughtai, Hans Raj Rahbar etc. for its development both in theme and form.

The partition of the country was a great event which brought untold misery and sufferings to the people of this sub-continent who had to leave their homes and migrate either to India or to Pakistan. This tragic event shook the old Hindu-Muslim amity which took shape through centuries and created a tot of social, economic and cultural problems e.g.

1. Husley, Aldous : Literature and Modern Life "International Literary Seminar", New Delhi, Sahitya Akademi, 1961, p. 8.

the clossal transfer of population, widespread communal riots, Kidnapping and abduction of girls, problem of rehabilitation and economic aid etc. The communal riots emerged as the main topic of the period. Qurratul Ain Haider, Balwant Singh, Ramanand Sagar, etc. produced some of the impressive novels which stood the challenge of the communal riots admirably well. In fact, in the following days quite a number of urdu novelists has chosen to write consistently about the common elements in Hindu and Muslim cultures and continued to emphasise upon secularism, humanism, and social justice. Qurratul Ain Haider's 'Mere Bhi Sanam Khane' is one of the most popular novels of that period in which she has discussed about those traditions of Indian culture which united the people of this subcontinent. But with the partition of the country communal riots broke out on a large scale and swept away all those emotional integrations which existed between Hindus and Muslims. In the same way Balwant Singh's 'Kale Kos' stand as a terrible reminder of the hells let loose in the Punjab at the time of the fateful partition of India. The arbitrary cutting of the country into two wings was an act of evil, and evil engendered more and still more evil. Once the seed of communal difference had been sown, how one could escape the whirlwind that uprooted masses of humanity. But man's normal nature is love which always guides him to a right path. Mian Dil Mohmmad saved Govindi—a Sikh girl who was Kidnapped, while going to India, by a Muslim mob. Ramanand Sagar, too, has written on communal riots and the problems that came with them. His famous novel 'Aur Insan Mar Gaya' is a fascinating sturdy of a sensitive soul, torn in tumult of the communal riots of 1947 and represents a firm and study humanist approach to the mass hysteria during those gloomy days.

Another dominant theme of urdu novels of this period was the portrayal of decaying feudal society especially Muslim feudal society, which was facing a new challenge due to the abolition of Zamindari system. A large number of Muslim landlords migrated to Pakistan to escape from the deteriorating socio-economic conditions. Most of the prominent urdu novelists such as Qurratul Ain Haider, Ismat Chughtai, Qazi Abdus Sattar wrote master piece novels related to social, economic and psychological problems of the Muslim feudal class. In other words such novels truly depicted 'the decline and fall of the feudal order against the background of the changing rural life of the eastern part of Uttar Pradesh.

One of the most striking trends in urdu novels is the portrayal of life and problems of people living in urban areas. India still lives in villagas but majority of urdu novelists have diverted their entire attentions towards the urban life and most of the characters of their novels are found in the urban setting. Among the exceptions Premchand is most eminent. He has given a new trend of thought and expression to urdu novel by introducing his readers to the rural life and problems such as poverty, caste differences, religious institutions and the sexual taboos etc. His novels reveal his deep sense of observation of the various socio-economic forces of the Indian rural society. After the partition of the country the life and problems of the rural life has increased but they have been neglected by the novelists. Other than Premchand the name of Qazi Abdus Sattar can also be mentioned for depicting the rural life in his novels. His novels entitled, 'Shab Gazida' and 'Pahla Aur Akhri Khat' depict the stories of Muslim landlords in the background of rural life.[2]

With the achievement of independence the foundation of a new pattern of socialistic society based on democracy, secularism, and social justice has been laid in India. After Independence the social mobilization has been accelerated. "It is the process in which major clusters of old social, economic and psychological commitments are eroded or broken and people become available for new patterns of socialization and behaviour."[3] The casual factors behind the uprooting of

2. Hassan, Mohammad, 'Indian Literature Since Independence' Ed. by Srinivasa Iyengar : New Delhi, Sahitya Akademi, 1973, p. 350.
3. Karl, W. Deutsch : "Social Mobilization and Political Development" in 'The Politics of Modernization', Chicago, The Univ. of Chicago, 1966, p. 582-603.

people from traditional modes of social and political behaviour are a variety of social forces viz. the growth of mass media, higher literacy, increasing urbanization, wider net works of transport and communication, greater geographical mobility, commercialization and industrialization etc. As a matter of fact the novelists in this context require multidimensional approach to penetrate into the unknown and the neglected sphere of life. Before partition urdu novelists, except few, were concerned only with the limited subject matter e.g. love, beauty, women, social reform and humanism but the post independence era provided them with several directions and dimensions of the problems confronted by the society and the people.

During the period under study the influence of Marxian ideology is obviously marked on the urdu novels and it started in 1938 but It became more apparent in the post independent period. The noted writers in the group are Khaja Ahmad Abbas, Krishan Chandar and few others. According to the Marxian ideology the economic foctors are the determinants of belief, thought, philosophy, literature, art and the like and reflect the position of the individuals in their class structure. Karl Marx has given the most forecful expression in his theory that the motive forces originate from the economic system and the thought as well as the actions of the individuals are conditioned accordingly. The different social groups have diverse economic interests and different motives and the course of history is determined by the struggle for power among these groups. According to him the history of man kind is, "a history of class struggles, contests between exploiting and exploited, ruling and oppressed classes."[4] As a matter of fact the Marxian ideology has also influenced the Indian writers and a group of urdu novelists have come forward to identify themselves as the believers of this ideology and written some master-piece novels, though the number of such novels are few, which reflect the Marxian ideology. Krishnn Chandar's famous novel 'Jab Khet Jage' depicts the

4. Engeles, Frederick, Preface, in Kari Marx's, 'The Communist Manifesto, Chicago', Henry Regnery, 1965, p. 7.

story of the struggle between Zamindars and Kisans of Telengana in South India. In the same way he has written more than a dozen novels of different length such as 'Ek Ladki Hazar Diwane', 'Dil Ki Wadian Sogaeen', 'Meri Yadon Ke Chonar', 'Sarak Wapas Jati Hai', 'Dader Pul Ke Buchche', etc. All these novels reveal a deep sense of economic and social awareness of the changing Indian Society. He is very much intesested with the problems of middle class people and criticises the bourgeois class for exploiting the poor people. Khaja Ahmad Abbas, a noted journalist and fiction writer, also accommodates the Marxian ideology in his novels. For instance his famous novel "Bombay Raat Ki Bahoon Me", depicts the story of exploitation of a poor journalist by a capitalist of Bombay. Through the character of Sona Das Daleria, the author has attempted to reveal the realistic picture of the social norms and economic affluence of the class of bourgeois living in the city of Bombay. On the other hand the character of Amar Kumar represents the poor section of the Indian journalist who has to face not only economic hardship but also the barriers to upward movement in the society created by the capitalist in our country.

The impact of Freudian idea is also marked in the novels of this period. The psycho-analytical approach to human behaviour has immensely influenced the contemporary literary mind. As a matter of fact modern writers have realised that a psychologically accurate account of what man is at any given moment can be given neither in terms of a static description of his character nor in terms of a group of chronologically arranged reactions to a series of circumstances. They have become interested in those aspects of consciousness which can not be viewed as progression of individual and self existing moments, but which are essentially dynamic rather than static in nature and are independent of the given moment. Novelists who employ the 'Stream of Consciousness' treat the character as a process not a state and present it outside time and place, in the double sense; firstly, they separate the presentation of consciousness from the chronological sequence of events, and secondly, they enable the quality of a given state of mind to be investigated so completly, by means of pursuing to their end the remote mental associations and suggestions, that we do not need to wait for time to make the potential actual before we can see the whole.

The application of psychological technique in novels is the outcome of Freudian impact on literature. Qurratul Ain Haider's 'Ag Ka Darya' is a very good example of 'Stream of consciousness' in urdu novels. She broke the traditional way of describing fictional themes with narrative formula and introduced a new technique by which the characters are presented outside time and place and not in a chronological series of events. The story starts from 2500 years back and gives the descriptions of Sravasti and Patliputra, two ancient seats of Indian culture and civilization; speaks about the arrival of Muslims in India and their downfall; throws light on rising power of the East India Company in India; and discusses the partition of India and the situations thereafter. There are only four central characters viz. Gautam, Harishankar, Champa and Kamal. They always take their births in different ages, but their characters and their instincts as well as emotions are the same.

Sex in one form or another has always been the main theme of most fictions, but the physical aspect of sex was covercd under some kind of spiritual cloak and there was no frankness in describing the sex or affairs related to it. The fiction writers, generally, used to describe 'love' as some thing mysterious. But under the influence of Freudian psychology this mysterious concepts of 'sex' or 'love' has been replaced by the frank and factual discussions of the physical aspects of sex. The writers belonging to Freueian school or in other words those writers influenced by the psycho-analytical approach of Freud believe that they are not reformers. It is true but they can avoid observing with critical eyes, and they have found it impossible to give their support to the conventional sexual morality or to speak highly of the means by which society attempts to control the practical problems of sex in human life. It can be demonstrated with ease that the morality demands more sacrifices than its worth, and bahaviour that follows is neither dictated by honesty nor instituted with wisdom. "The writers do not absolve their patience from listening to these criticism they accustom them to unprejudiced consideration of sexual matters like all other matters; and if, after they have become independent by the effect of the treatment, they chose some intermediate course between unrestrained sexual licence and unconditional, ascetius, their conscience is not bothered whatever the outcome."[5]

As a matter of fact sex as the chief motive force in human behaviour is the dominant theme of modern urdu novels. The modern writers discuss sex quite frankly instead of feeling shy or guilty about it, Sex is no more a taboo. Earlier urdu novelists depicted sexual themes in restricted way and they did not portray the sexual aspects of their characters in the novels because the temperament of the society at that time was based on religious and spiritual values. For instance Moulvi Nazir Ahmad and Rashidul Khairi wrote only about moral and social themes and did not depict the sexual behaviour or the problems related to sex in human life in their novels. Freudian concept however, exerted a powerful influence on literary minds in the post independence period. Urdu novelists deviated from the treditional way of thinking and made themselves from ethical boundage to accept new trends of life. Writers like Aziz Ahmad, Krishan Chandar, Ismat Chughtai, Mahindar Nath, Balwant Singh etc. were influenced by Freudian idea. For instance, Aziz Ahmad in his famous novel 'Aisi Bulandi Aisi Pasti' presented a picture of sexual life of the bourgieoise living in the city of Hyderabad in Daccan. Ismat Chughtai's famous novel 'Masooma' depicted the sexual life of upper class people of Bombay. In the same way Mahindar Nath's novels 'Aadmi Aur Sikka', 'Raat Andheri Hai' etc. portrayed the sexual life and problems related to sex in contemporary Indian Society.

The influence of Freudian concept, thus, has brought about radical changes not only in the structure of urdu novels but the substance has also changed. The modern writers bring to fiction, among their own individual qualities, a new realism

5. Quoted by Raj Kumar "The New Morality in Modern Fiction" Delhi, Jiwan Prakashan, p. 92.

in which the reflection or interpretation of life, and not the manipulation of it, is of the first importance. The novelist is not at all concerned about the goodness, beauty or ugliness of his remarkable world, but he is concerned to show that it is like that. His purpose is not to exaggerate rather to describe exactly what human beings are like. He is more interested in the study of inner life of individuals in a given society. His personality, motivation and attitudes are determined by the social order. According to Erick Fromm, 'Man as he appears in any given culture is always manifestation of human nature, a manifestation, however, which in its specific outcome is determined by social arrangements under which he lives."[6] Thus the aim of the modern urdu novelists is to come as near as possible to the reality of human life. That is why the modern urdu novel has attained a seriousness and is no longer content to remain merely a source of amusement for the idle hour. The modern reader has also become more subtle. He no longer reads novel just to amuse himself or to escape but to find the inner truth of life. He wants from the novelists not only an outside photograph but a portrait of the whole man. In the works of new writers there is a scientific precision in the dissection of ordinary mental processes like anxiety, anger, frustration, introspection, memory, perception sensation, sublimation etc. Similarly when the novelist deals with the topics like environment, heredity, sex, crime, punishment, etc. he does so from the scientific and objective angles.

The process of liberation is a basic social trend in post independent India. The rigid hierarchial structure of our society is fast breaking up. This is the consequences of the rapid process of modernization and also of democratic constitution we have given to ourselves. This has brought about a distinct qualitative change in the attitudes, responses, and behaviour which is inevitably being reflected in the literature. Certain economic changes are affecting the family structure and women are exposed to a new chellenge in a new

6. Fromm : Erick. 'The Sane Society', New York, Rinehart & Co, In 1955, p. 14.

society. In this new society the environment is more liberal and the opportunities are infinite. As a matter of fact women are trying to be benefited from this new atmosphere and girls are being given modern education. It is the pressure both economic and social, which has led women to enter into gainful employment and it has created a feeling of independence within women. Now they are playing an increasingly important part in social life. The most remarkable feature of urdu novels is the female characters which reflect the tunes of the changing Indian society. For instance the female characters like Rakhshanda Begum (Mere Bhi Sanam Khane) Mohindar Kaur (Kale Kos), Azra (Azra), Suman (Suman) etc. tell us of the growing consciousness of the changing position and status of females in the contemporary society. But the Indian womenhood has yet to cover a longway to achieve a dignified position as well as mancipation. The society still stores sufficient sorrows and exploitations for them.

There is a marked increase in the number of women novelists in urdu literature. This is because of the rapid development of female education and democratic set up of the Indian society. Among them the names of Ismat Chughtai, Qurratul Ain Haider, Saleha Abid Hussain, Razia Sajjad Zaheer, etc. are worth mentioning. These writers have tried to portrary the female characters in the context of changing Muslim Society of India. Their novels reveal a wide range of subjects covering love, sex, social problems, politics, economic conditions, the fading world of the past and the challenges of the modern society etc.

Industrialization and urbanization have brought about new opportunities and challenges in the post independent India. It has changed the destiny of Indian people by raising the standard of living, increasing production and offering opportunities, but on the other hand, it has created socio-economic problems, bureaucratic corruption and nepotism etc. This new situation has also helped the development of new modes of expression and new techniques in literature including urdu novels. Most of the novelists of this period have depicted the socio-economic and psychological problems emerging due to the rapid increase in industrialization and urbanization in India. The growing rate of cities and out-throat competition therein have created an environment which is hostile to human life. Slums are producing an explosive tension-ridden atmosphere in which a large number of people spend their entire lives. This challenging situation of a country like India has attracted the writers to portray the alarming condition of the people living in the slums. Khaja Ahmad Abbas, Mahindar Nath, Hansraj Rahbar etc. have depicted the miserable conditions of slums in India. Khaja Ahmad Abbas's famous novel 'Bombay Raat Ki Bahon Me' gives a pathetic picture of slvm life of Bombay which is the outcome of present industrial and urdan growth. He has analysed various socio-economic factor which are responsible for such type of living condition in a big city. According to a study the total population living in the slums of Bombay is about 4.16 lakhs.[7] In the same way Mahindar Nath's 'Raat Andheri Hai' and Hansraj Rahbar's 'Parade Ground' depict some of the problems of people living in slums.

The increase in the number of reading public and the expansion in the publication of books have brought about a significant change in the Indian society. After the independence there has been a tremendous development of the mass market for books. This is due to the fact that the bulk of nation's population has attained literacy. Due to the changes in the literacy situation that have occurred within past two decades, the market for literary works and especlally novels expanded from a very limited section of the population to the vast bulk of it. Not, of course, that any and all literary products would now find a mass market but such a market is for the first time potentially available. The authors have now gradually reached the point where they can address a large body of readers who are sufficiently cultivated to welcome and purchase a variety of literary products. Thus with the increasing professionalization of literary activity, writers find it possible and worthwhile to devote more time and effort to their writing. There

7. Bombay Municipal Corporation (1956-57), in 'Slums and Urbanization' Ed. by A R. Desai and S. Peredas Pillai, Bombay, Popular Prakashan, 1970, p. 155.

is also a keener competition to gct published and catch the attention of the reading public. As a result there is a distinct improvement in the competence with which the fiction is written. During the period, under review, urdu novelists also have come up to meet the needs of the literary market. Conseqently, a group of professional novelists have emerged. Among them the names of Krishan Chandar, K.A. Abbas, Qurratul Ain Haider, Gulshan Nanda, Nasim Anhonvi, Dat Bharti, Jamna Das Akhtar, Adil Rashid, Arif Mahrurvi, Akhtar Maleehabadi, Gopal Krishna, Abid Zia Azimabadi, Qaisi Rampuri etc. are worthmentioning. But at the same time this commercialization of urdu novels has brought unhealthy effects. It has resulted in a lot of writing that is vulgar and debased. Most of the novels are based on sex, crime and violence.

Mostly urdu novels of this period depict the characters of middle class people and very few novels touch the life and problems of upper class society. For instance the novels of Quratul Ain Haider, Qazi Abdus Sattar, Ismat Chughtai etc. portray the life and problems of upper ciass people. It indicates that the popular novels of our age are more related to common people and reflect mass culture by describing the characters of common people of the society.

There is something common in the worlds of experience of all the outstanding younger writers of urdu fiction. They convey a sense of chaos, frustration and disintegration. This is partly a reflection of the contemporary social situation. It is something deeprooted and therefore of considerable literary value.

Before concluding this chapter it would be wise to point out the various socio-economic and psychological factors affecting the development of urdu novels in the post independent India. There is no doubt that urdu novels during this period made sufficient development both in themes and experessions. But in comparison to other forms of literature, especially poetry and short stories, novel has not gained much popularity.

Some of the factors that proved detrimental to the development of the novel are undoubtedly economic. Urdu writers can not depend, except few, solely on writing for a livelihood. Very few of them can devote even a substantial part of their time to it. This is one of the reasons why the short stories have flourished more than the novels. Eminent urdu novelists in most cases were attached to the film industry for their livelihood by writing film scripts and dialogues. Among them Krishan Chandar, Khaja Ahmad Abbas, Rajindar Singh Bedi, Gulshan Nanda are worth mentioning. On the other hand the economic background of the Muslim community is far from satisfactory. They can purchase journals but seldom they purchase novels. Thus the urdu writers work in a community where the standard of living is low and the percentage of literacy is not very encouraging.

Mostly the books in urdu this Seventies were printed through lithography where publishers were dependent on 'Katib' (one who copies manuscripts in their handwritings). As a result there were more chances of delay in publishing the materials as well as committing mistakes. This lengthy process involves extra money, energy and time. Hence the pirnting problem has also affected the popularity of novels in urdu literature. However, Lithography is being replaced by other modern technologies of printing).

Another factor which deserves mention is the cultural tradition. Poetry in fact enjoys a higher prestige than prose in urdu and men possessing creative talent apply it accordingly. Mushairas (Poetic gatherings) are still very much liked by common people and is regarded as the real creative work.

Finally, the popularity of short stories has also posed a challenge to the development of urdu novels. Most of the urdu novelists are eminent short story writers too.

However, inspite of various shortcomings the present treasure of urdu novels is not very discouraging. It has successfully reflected the cnanging vision of our contemporary society. The attempt of the modern novelists to convey the stuff of life by capturing the actual moment of it has influenced the novel in a number of ways.

Select Bibliography

Ahmed, Aziz, Islamic Modernity in India and Pakistan, Oxford University Press, London, 1967.

Ahmad, Zazir., Lecture on Mossalmanon Ki Halate Talim, Quoted by Tarachand, History of the Freedom Movement in India, Publication Division, Govt. of India, New Delhi, 1967.

Albrecht, M.C., Does Literature Reflected Common Values ? American Sociological Review, 21 (1956).

Alexander, F. and Ross, H., Dynamic Psychiatry, Univ. of Chicago Press, Chicago, 1952.

Allen, W., Reading a Novel, Phonix House, London, 1949.

Asch, S.E., Social Psychology, Prentice-Hall, New York, 1922.

Ansari, Iqbal, Muslim and The National Integration, Radiane, New Delhi, 1969.

Azad, Muhammad Hussain, Abe Hayat, Ehsan Book Depot.

Barelson, B. and N. Salter, P., Minority and Majority Americans An analysis of Magazine Fiction, Public Opinion, Quarterly, 10(1946).

Bargel, E.E., Prolegomena to Sociology of art in 'Towards Sociology of Culture in India', Ed. by T.K.N. Unnithan *et. al.* Prentice Hall of India (Pvt.) Ltd., New Delhi, 1965.

Battelhein, Charles, India Independent (English translation by W.A. Caswell) Maegibbon and Kee, London, 1968.

Becker, H. and Boskoff, A. (Ed.), Modern Sociological theory in continuity and change, Essay entitled, Sociology, of Art, Literature and Music by Hugh, D. Duncan, Rinehart and Winston, New York, 1957.

Bernett, J.H. and Guren, R., Recent American Divorce Novels, Social Forces, 26(1948).

Biersted, R. (Ed.), The making of society, The Modern Library, New York, 1959.

Biswas, D.K., Sociology of Major Bengali Novels, The Academic Press, Gurgaon, 1974.

Burke, K., A Grammer of Motives, Prentice Hall, New York, 1945.

Britt, A.A., Social Psychology of Modern Life Hall Rinehart, New York.

Britt, A.A., Freud's Contribution to Psychaitry. Norton and Co., London, 1941.

Census Report Government of India, New Delhi, 1951.

Clark, T.W., The Novel in India; Its birth and development, Essay entitled, The Modern Novel in Urdu by Russel R. George Allen and Unwin Ltd., London, 1970.

Cooley, C.H., Social Organisation, Charles Scribner's Sons, New York, 1909.

Desai, A.R. and Pillai, S.P., Slums and Urbanization, Popular Prakashan, Bombay, 1970.

Deutsch, K.W., Social Mobilization and Political development, University of Chicago Press, Chicago, 1966.

Devanandan, P.V. and Thomas, M.M. (Ed.), Christian Participation in Nation Building, National Christian Council and Christian Institute for the Study of Religion and Sociology, Bangalore, 1960.

Dubey, S.C., Men's and Women's Role in India : A Sociological Review—taken from Women in the New Asai, edited by Barbara, E. Ward, UNESCO, Paris, 1965.

Duhany, Don, E. (Ed.), Contribution to modern Psychology. Oxford Press, New York.

Election Manifesto of Indian National Congress, 1951.

Encyclopedia Americana, American Corporation, 1966.

Encyclopedia Britanica, Oxford University Press, London, 1965.

Engeles, F., Preface in Karl Marx's The Communist Manifesto, Henry Regnery, Chicago, 1965.
Farooqui, A., Urdu Novel Ki Tanquidee Tareekh.
Fielder, L. (Ed.), The Art of the Essay : Essay entitled, That Art of Fiction by Walter Peasant.
Fox, Ralph., Novel and The People. Foreign Language Publishing House, Moscow, 1964.
Freud, A., The Ego and the Mechanism of defence, The Hograth Press and the Institution of Psycho-Analysis, London, 1954.
Freud, S., Civilization and 25 Discontent. Hograth Press, London, 1956.
Freud, S., A New Series of Introductory lectures on Psycho-analysis, Norton, London, 1933.
Freud, S., Delusion and dream and other essays, Relcon Press, Boston, 1956.
Freud, S., The complete introductory lectures on Psycho-analysis. George Allen and Unwin, London, 1971.
Fromm, E., The Same Society, Rinehart and Co., New York, 1955.
Gazetteer of India, Vol. II-Country and People, New Delhi Publication Division, Govt. of India, 1966.
Gillin, J.L. and Gillin, J.P., Cultural Sociology, Macmillan, New York, 1954.
Ghosh, Alak, Indian Economy : Its Nature and Problems, World Press (P.) Ltd., Calcutta, 1968.
Goode, W J. and Hatt, P.K., Methods in Social Research, McGraw-Hill, New York, 1952.
Graudy, Rogers, Marxism in the Twentieth Century (Translated by Rene Hague) Collins, London, 1970.
Grierson, George Abraham, Linguistic Survey of India, Vol. I Part I, Govt. of India, Central Publication Branch, Calcutta, 1927.
Hedlbroner, R.L., The worldly philosophers, Simon and Schuster, New York, 1953.
Hendwick, Ives., Theories of Psycho-analysis, Alfred A. Knoff, New York, 1958.
Hippolyte, History of English Literature. Henry Holt, New York, 1886.

Hudson, H.V., The great divide : Britain—India-Pakistan, Hutchins, London, 1969.

Hudson, W.T., An introduction to the study of Literature, George G. Harper, London, 1958.

Huxley, Aldox, Literature and Modern Life. International Literary Seminar, Sahitya Akademi, New Delhi, 1961.

Illyas Barani., Marrif-i-Millat, Aligarh, 1924.

India : A Statistical Outline, Oxford and IBH Publishing Co., Calcutta, 1974.

Inglis, R., An objective Approach to the Relationship between fiction and society, American Sociological Review, 3:4 (1938).

Institute of Advanced Studies, Simla Modernity and Contemporary in India Literature : Essay by Surooy, A.A. entitled in contemporary Urdu poetry; Simla, 1968.

Institute of Advanced Studies, Simla Language and Society in India—Essays by Zaidi, S.K. entitled Urdu in India, Simla, 1969.

Irvine, Later Mughals.

Iyengar, Srinivas (Ed.), Indian Literature Since Independence, Essay by Mohammad Hassan. Sahitya Akademy, New Delhi, 1973.

Jones, E., The Life and Work of Sigmund Freud, Vol. 3, Basic Book Inc., New York, 1957.

Kabir, H., The Indian Heritage, Asia, Delhi, 1955.

Kapur, Promilla, Marriage and the Working Women in India, Vikas Publications, Delhi, 1970.

Kine, P., Fact and Fantasy in Freudian Theory, Methuen and Co., London, 1972.

Klein and Others, Development in Psycho-analysis. The Hograth Press, London, 1952.

Kolaja, Jiri and Wilson R.N., The Themes of Social Isolation in American Painting and Poetry, Aesthetics and Art Criticism.

Krech, D. and Crutchfield, The Theory and Problems of Social Psychology, McGraw-Hill, New York, 1948.

Kripal, Prem., A Decade of Education, Indian Book Co., Delhi, 1968.

Kumar, R., The New Morality in Modern Fiction, Jiwan Prakashan, Delhi.

Lichthein, George, Marxism, A Historical and Cultural Study, Routledge and Kegan Paul London, 1961.

Lord, Palmerston., Debate in the British Parliament. (Commons) Vide Hausard 12.2,1858.

Lowenthal, L., Literature and Image of Man. Beacon Press, 1957.

Lundberg, G.A., Social Research, Longmans, Green and Co. New York, 1942.

MacIver, R.M. and Page, C.H., Society. Macmillan, London, 1955.

Malaviya, H.D., Land Reform in India, New Delhi, 1955.

Mallik, B.N., My Years with Nehru : The Chinese Betrayal, Allied, Bombay, 1971.

Mallik, Amita, Article entitled, Women and Politics Sundary Hindustan Standard Colour Magazine, Dated 23-7-1973. Calcutta.

Marx, K. and Engles F., Selected Works, Vol. II, Foreign Language Publishing House, Moscow, 1955.

Marx, Engels, Lenin., The Essential Left. Unwin Books, London, 1950.

Marx, K. Engels, F., Literature and Art, International Publishers, New York, 1947.

Mellor, Andrew, India Since Partition, Trustile Press, London, 1951.

Menon, V.P., The Transfer of Power in India, Orient Longmans, Bombay, 1957.

Merton, R.K. (Ed.), Sociology Today : Problem and Prospects. Essays Entitled, 'The Sociology of Art' by James H. Barnett, Basic Book Inc., New York, 1959.

Mosley, Leonard, The Last Days of British Raj. Hascourt, New Yark, 1961.

Mukherji, B., Objectives and Methods of Community Development—taken from extension Education in Community Development, Directorate of Extension, Ministry of Food and Agriculture, Govt. of India, New Delhi, 1961.

Mukherjee, R.N., A History of Social Thought. Saraswati Prakashan, Mussorie, 1960.

Nagendra (Ed.), Indian Literature : Essay by Faroqui, K.A, Sahitya Akademi, New Delhi.

Ogbum, W.F. and Nimkoff, M.F., A Hand Book of Sociology, Routledge and Kegan Paul, London, 1950.

O'Mally, L.S.S., Modern India and The West, Oxford University Press, London, 1941.

Pannikar, K.M., The Foundation of New India. George Allen and Unwin, 1963.

Reminiscences of Karl Marx an essay by Engels entitled, Karl Marx, wrirten in June, 1877, Published in the Volk Kalendar, an almanac which appeared in Burnsurick in 1877, Foreign Language Publishing House, Moscow.

Rosenblatt, Louis, M., Literature as exploitation, Heinemann Educational Book Ltd; London, 1958.

Savarkar, V.P., Hindi Rashtra Darshan, L.G. Khare and Sons, Bombay, 1949.

Saxena, K.C., Pakistan, her relation with India (1947-1966), Vir Publishing House, New Delhi, 1966.

Saxena, Rambabu., A History of Urdu Literature. Ram Narain Lall, Allahabad, 1927.

Schlesinger, Rudolf Marx, his time and hours. Routledge and Kegan Paul, London, 1951.

Segal, Ronald., The Crisis of India, Jaico Publishing House, Bombay, 1968.

Schramm, Wilbur, Mass Media and National Development. Sanford University Press, Sanford, 1967.

Seligman, E.R.A. and Johnson, A., Selection from the Encyclopedia of Social Sciences, The Macmillan and Co., New York, 1959.

Shakir, Moin, Muslim in Free India, Kalankar Prakashan, New Delhi, 1972.

Sheriff, M. and Sheriff, C.W., An outline of Social Psychology, Harper, New York, 1956.

Sills, D.L. (Ed.), Encyclopedia of the Social Science Vol. 13, Macmillan, New York, 1968.

Smith, L. and Strouss, Social Psychology. Holt-Rinehart and Winston, New York, 1956.

Smith, D.E., India—A Secular State. Princeton University, London, 1967.

Smith, V.A., Oxford History of India. Oxford University, London, 1958.

Spencer, H., The Principles of Psychology. Appleton, New York, 1882.

Sorokin, P., Contemporary Sociological Theories. Harper and Row. Publisher, New York, 1964.

Sorokin, P., Social and Cultural Dynamics, America Book, New York, 1937.

Sriniwas, M.N., Social Change in Modern India. Allied Publisher, Bombay, 1966.

Suroor, A.A., Aligarh History of Urdu Literature essay by Masood Hussain Khan, Aligarh, 1962.

Thomas, P., Indian Women Through the Ages, Asia, Bombay, 1964.

Turner, Roy (Ed.), India's Urban Future. Oxford University Press, Bombay, 1962.

Tyson, Geofrey, Nehru—The Years of Power. Pall Mall Press, London, 1966.

Warren, Austin and Wellek, Rene., Theory of Literature. Jonathan Kar, London, 1954.

Index